No-Miss Lessons
for
Preteen Kids

Group
Loveland, Colorado

No-Miss Lessons for Preteen Kids

Credits
Thanks to all the authors who have contributed great lessons to Junior High Ministry Magazine and Children's Ministry Magazine over the years.
Editor: Mary Van Aalsburg
Managing Editor: Paul Woods
Chief Creative Officer: Joani Schultz
Copy Editor: Julie Meiklejohn
Designer and Art Director: Jean Bruns
Cover Art Director: Helen H. Lannis
Cover Designer: Melanie Lawson
Computer Graphic Artist: Joyce Douglas
Cover Photographer: Craig DeMartino
Illustrator: Amy Bryant
Production Manager: Ann Marie Gordon

Unless otherwise noted, Scriptures quoted from The Youth Bible, New Century Version, copyright © 1991 by Word Publishing, Dallas, Texas 75039. Used by permission.

Library of Congress Cataloging-in-Publication Data
No-miss lessons for preteen kids / [from the editors of] Group Publishing.
   p. cm.
  ISBN 0-7644-2015-1
  1. Christian education of children. 2. Church work with children.
3. Children—Religious life. 4. Children—Conduct of life.
I. Group Publishing.
BV1475.2.N6 1997
268'.432—dc20
        96-35339
        CIP

10 9 8 7 6 5 4 3 2   06 05 04 03 02 01 00 99 98 97
Printed in the United States of America.

Contents

Introduction

Are your preteen kids bored with those same old Bible stories? Having trouble holding kids' interest and getting them involved? Are you looking for lessons that grab kids' interest and leave them wanting more?

Welcome to the club! Keeping preteen kids interested in church activities is, at best, a challenge. Never fear, help is on the way! *No-Miss Lessons for Preteen Kids* is full of lessons that will grab kids' attention and keep them coming back for more.

Kids are growing up faster than ever. Interests, fears, needs, and pressures that we used to ascribe to junior or senior high school students are now the topics at the lunchroom table of our fifth- and sixth-grade kids. These kids are growing up in a world where things move faster, loom larger, and push harder than ever before. The lessons in this book will help kids know that they have a solid rock of safety and a place they can turn for help, advice, and love.

In *No-Miss Lessons for Preteen Kids,* you'll find attainable goals for each lesson combined with fun, active learning that is focused on faith, self, relationships, issues, and service. Each lesson is based on Scripture and gives you, as the leader, options to set the tempo of the lessons and to effectively close your time together.

Kids need to know that they are of value—to you, to their families, to their world, and especially, to God. *No-Miss Lessons for Preteen Kids* provides lots of fun ways to reinforce that truth. The added Bonus Ideas section helps you set up your group for service—at the church, in the neighborhood, or for the community. Included are twenty-five sure-fire projects to help your kids live out what they have been learning.

Don't wait any longer! Pick a topic, gather those ten-to-twelve-year-olds together, open your Bible, and have some fun.

Section 1:
Faith Foundations

Goal:

Know Jesus personally!

Scripture Verses:

1 John 1:5–2:6

Knowing Jesus

While a lot of kids know about Jesus, they don't really know him. And unfortunately, knowing about Jesus doesn't change kids' lives—or give them the promise of eternal life. Knowing Jesus does. Through this lesson, kids will have an opportunity to meet Jesus and have a visual reminder of God's revelations in their lives.

Choose Your Opening

❑ Option 1: Hairbrained Idea

(For this activity, you'll need an envelope and a pencil for each person.)

Give kids envelopes and pencils. Have each person pluck three to five hairs from his or her head and place them in an envelope. Kids should write their birthdays (just day and month) on the right-hand corner of their envelopes for identification purposes. Collect the envelopes, and mix them up.

Redistribute the envelopes so each person has someone else's envelope. Ask kids to examine the hair in the envelopes and see if they can determine who the hair belongs to. Have kids write the name of the person they think the hair belongs to on the outside of each envelope. Pass the envelopes around so each person can make a guess for every envelope.

Then have kids retrieve their own envelopes and tell the group how many right answers were recorded. Ask:

● **How easy was it to identify the people whose hair was in the envelopes?**

● **What was difficult about this activity?**

● **How is this activity like getting to know Jesus?**

Then say: **Just as it's difficult to know someone by a few hairs, we can't know Jesus if we see only a small part of him. One of the most important elements of our faith is the desire to know Jesus and to know him well. Today we'll explore how to know Jesus—and how to know we know him.**

❏ Option 2: Jesus Can

(For this activity, provide an unmarked tin can, ten index cards, and a sheet of construction paper for each person. Have scissors, markers, and tape available.)

Give each person an unmarked tin can, ten index cards, and a sheet of construction paper. Ask kids to write one thing they know about Jesus on each card. They may think of characteristics or names such as "loving," "forgiving," or "Lord." Have kids place the cards in their tin cans and make labels for the cans that describe the person they've described on their cards. They can use the construction paper, markers, and tape. For example, kids might write "King of Kings," "The Miracle Man," or "A Real Friend."

Have volunteers tell the group what they wrote on their cards. Remind kids not to judge each other's ideas but to listen and learn about each other's understanding of who Jesus is.

Form groups of no more than four, and have kids discuss the following questions:

● **What does this activity tell us about knowing Jesus?**
● **What did you learn about Jesus from someone else's card?**

Then say: **As you can see, we know many things about Jesus. However, there's a difference between knowing *about* Jesus and knowing him personally. Today you're going to learn how you can *know* Jesus—and know that you know him.**

The Bible Experience

How Do We Know?

(For this activity, write the names "Charles Manson," "Demi Moore," "Michael Jordan," and "Mariah Carey" on four separate paper plates. On a fifth plate write "Jesus, 1 John 1:5–2:6." Have a Bible available.)

Scatter the five paper plates face-down around the room. Ask kids each to move to a paper plate and stand on or near it. Have kids at each paper plate pick up the plate and silently read the name on it.

Have kids at each plate describe to the rest of the group how their lives would be different if they personally knew the person listed on their plate (without saying the name on the plate). For example, someone near the "Michael Jordan" plate might say, "I'd be famous if I knew this person" or "I'd probably become a better basketball player."

Then have the kids at that plate take turns answering the following questions:

● **How would your relationship with this person change your living conditions, free time, or group of friends?**
● **Would your parents approve of this relationship? Why or**

why not?

● **Would you want to grow to be more like this person? Explain.**

Continue having the kids at each plate tell about their person in this manner, and ask the kids standing near the "Jesus" plate to go last (remember where you placed this plate). Then have kids guess whose name is written on each plate. Ask:

● **What's the difference between *knowing about* someone and *having a relationship* with that person?**

Ask one of the kids near the "Jesus" plate to read aloud the passage listed on it (1 John 1:5–2:6). Then ask:

● **According to this passage, how do we come to know Jesus?**

● **How do we know if we know him?**

● **How does knowing Jesus change our lives?**

Say: **By confessing our sins, we begin a relationship with Jesus and come to know him. And by obeying Jesus' commands, we know that we know him.**

Reflection and Application

Getting to Know Him

(For this activity, you'll need the Jesus plate from the "How Do We Know?" activity.)

Place the Jesus plate face-up in the center of the room. Have kids form a circle around the plate, and ask volunteers to share how knowing Jesus has made a difference in their lives. If kids aren't sure what to say, you might want to share how knowing Jesus has affected your life.

Say: **Some of you may know a lot *about* Jesus but not yet know him personally. Let's take a few moments to silently consider our relationships with Jesus.**

Give kids the opportunity to publicly express their desire to know Jesus or to grow in their relationship with Christ by standing next to the Jesus plate. If kids do step forward, lead the rest of the group in praying that those people will come to know Jesus better.

Let kids know that they can talk to you further after the lesson if they have questions about what it means to know Jesus.

Choose Your Closing

❏ Option 1: How We've Come to Know Jesus

(For this activity, you'll need a ten-inch piece of cord or heavy yarn for each student.)

Ask kids to think about different ways they've come to know Jesus. Answers might include "learning at church," "seeing Jesus' love in others," "reading the Bible," or "being taught by the Holy Spirit."

Then give kids each a ten-inch piece of cord or heavy yarn, and say: **Tie a knot in this cord for each of three times in your life that you've come to know Jesus better. You might think of experiences when you were in crisis, times spent in prayer, or situations where a friend helped you see Jesus' love.**

Form trios, and have kids tell what their knots symbolize. Close the meeting by encouraging kids to use their cords as bookmarks, and remind them to add a knot each time God helps them grow significantly in their relationships with Jesus.

❏ Option 2: Know Way

(For this activity, you'll need a piece of poster board and several markers.)

Have someone in your group who has good handwriting write the words "Know Way" on poster board. Then have kids each add to the sign by drawing a symbol or writing a word that describes what it's like to know Jesus.

Place the sign near the entrance to your classroom. Have kids take turns completing the following sentence: "We can make our classroom a place to know Jesus by..."

Close by having kids offer prayers asking God to help them grow closer to Christ and to share their knowledge of Christ with others.

Goal:
Love God!

Scripture Verses:
1 John 5:1-5; Matthew 10:37; 1 Corinthians 13:1-13; and 1 Peter 1:8

Loving Jesus

So much babble about love on television, in music, at home, and in the church: "I love the way you did your hair…" "I'm in love with…" "You'll really love this new car…" "We should love Jesus with all our heart…" Yet how is anyone supposed to know what love is really all about?

With this lesson you'll help kids learn what it means to love Jesus and discover what Jesus means when he commands us to love.

Choose Your Opening

❏ Option 1: Love Operation

(For this activity, select three outgoing kids to play the parts of Dr. Brain, Dr. Heart, and Dr. Stomach. They will each be trying to convince the group that love is centered in the part of the body they're representing.)

Ask for a volunteer to participate in a brief improvised skit. Have that person lie down on a table or couch. Say: **We have a bit of a problem here. Our volunteer needs to have his** (or her) **love removed for a checkup, but I'm not sure where to look to find it. So I've invited three specialists to see if they can find the patient's love and remove it.**

Invite the three doctors (Dr. Brain, Dr. Heart, and Dr. Stomach) to each describe the procedure they'd use to remove the person's love. Have each doctor tell where the love is located and why he or she thinks it's in that area of the body.

For example, Dr. Brain might explain that love is located in the brain because it's something intellectual. Or Dr. Heart might say it's located in the heart because it's an emotional thing. Dr. Stomach might explain that love is usually found in the stomach—the place where pizza ends up.

Encourage the doctors to outdo each other in their explanations. Then allow group members to ask questions of the doctors.

After the skit, say: **We hear the word "love" used for everything** from our favorite food to an expression of the relationship between two people about to be married. **But what is true love? And what does it mean to truly love Jesus? Today we'll explore the importance of loving Jesus.**

❏ Option 2: Extreme Love

Form a circle. Ask for a volunteer to go first in creating an extreme expression of love. To do this, the person will face someone in the circle and complete the following sentence: "My love for you is…"

Have the volunteer complete the sentence with a comparison such as "…as deep as the ocean" or "…as mushy as day-old oatmeal." Then the person he or she is speaking to must counter with his or her own outrageous expression of love within seven seconds. If this person can't respond with a new expression of love within the time limit, he or she must take the place of the first volunteer and face someone else in the circle. Encourage kids to outdo one another with outrageous comparisons (humorous or just plain hard-to-believe).

After the game, say: **We've had a little fun playing with the idea of love. But what does love really look like? And how can we express love in our relationships with Jesus? Today we'll explore why it's important to love Jesus—and how to show our love to him.**

The Bible Experience

Solid as a Rock

(For this activity, you'll need one Bible for each group. Write the following Scripture references on a sheet of paper: Matthew 10:37; 1 Corinthians 13:1-13; 1 Peter 1:8; and 1 John 5:1-5. Fold the paper, and place it under a large rock in the center of your classroom so that it can't be seen.)

Form groups of no more than four. Have groups form a circle around the rock. Then say: **Soon I'm going to assign each of you a Scripture passage that sheds some light on what love is and how we're supposed to love Jesus. But first take a couple of minutes to brainstorm what you think might be under this rock.**

After groups brainstorm what they think is under the rock, have a volunteer from each group share the group's ideas. Ask:
● **What's it like to guess what might be under this rock?**
● **How is the way you guessed about what is under the rock like the way some people approach a relationship with Jesus?**
● **What's the best way to find out what's under this rock?**

Have kids move the rock. Then pick up the paper, and assign a Scripture passage from the list to each group. Distribute the Bibles. Have

kids in each group look up and read their passage and then determine what it says about love (loving Christ, loving others, or love in general). After five minutes or so, have groups tell what they discovered.

Now have kids discuss the following questions in their groups:

● **What "rocks" in our lives do we have to remove to love Jesus?**

● **What keeps us from loving Jesus more?**

● **According to the Bible, why is it important to love God?**

● **What are practical ways to help our love for God to grow?**

Have volunteers tell about their groups' insights. Then say: **Love is a difficult concept to understand. But the Bible gives us a good picture of love. And it tells us that loving God should be one of our utmost goals. Let's use the next activity to examine ways to demonstrate our love for Jesus.**

Reflection and Application

Rocky Love

(For this activity, you'll need a Bible, a rock, newsprint, and a marker.)

Before your meeting, write the important phrases from 1 Corinthians 13 on newsprint.

Read 1 Corinthians 13 aloud to the kids. Then say: **Let's practice demonstrating our love by using this rock as the object of our love.**

Give kids four minutes to express their love for the rock through their words or actions. Remind kids to use the 1 Corinthians 13 definition of love, rather than the world's definition of love.

After four minutes, ask:

● **What was it like to demonstrate love toward a rock?**

● **How is this like the way God might feel when he demonstrates love toward people who don't respond?**

● **How did God demonstrate his love for us?**

● **How can we respond to God's love?**

Form groups of no more than four, and have kids brainstorm ways to express love to Jesus as well as to each other. Encourage kids to come up with practical ideas, such as a random act of kindness for a person needing a helping hand. Have volunteers from each small group tell their ideas to the whole group.

Choose Your Closing

❑ Option 1: Love Calls

(For this activity, have a disconnected telephone available.)

Place the telephone in the center of the room, and have kids form a circle around it. Say: **Let's imagine that Jesus is going to call us on this phone in just a couple of minutes. He's going to ask us about our love for him and for those around us. Spend the next few minutes in silence, imagining what you might say to Jesus.**

Allow a couple of moments for reflection, then have volunteers close the meeting by praying that group members would learn to love Jesus fully and to love others with a Christlike love.

❏ Option 2: Love in Any Language

(For this activity, tape a sheet of newsprint to the wall, and have markers and paper available.)

Say: **We can express our love to Jesus in many ways through our words and actions. To remind us of the importance of loving Jesus, we're going to create a unique picture that symbolizes our love.**

Have kids brainstorm symbols that could represent each of the letters in the phrase "I love Jesus." For example, someone might suggest a picture of an eye for the letter "I" or a heart shape for the letter "o." Then have kids draw the shapes on the newsprint to create a picture of their love for Jesus.

Have kids each copy the symbols onto a piece of paper to keep with them at school and at home. Encourage kids to use the symbols often as a reminder of the importance of loving Jesus and one another.

Close by having kids express their love for Jesus with one-word prayers acknowledging the characteristics of Jesus they most appreciate, such as "comfort," "peace," or "hope."

Goal:
Follow in Jesus' footsteps!

Scripture Verses:
1 John 3:7-10;
Matthew 4:18-19

Following Jesus

When we know and love Jesus, we must follow him. This means doing what's right in day-to-day living. Jesus calls all Christians to follow him—a task that's easier said than done in today's pressure- and pleasure-filled society. Kids will look at ways they're "called" to follow ideas, products, and people. They'll discover Jesus' call to follow him, learning that following Jesus means becoming more like him.

Choose Your Opening

❏ Option 1: Supermarket Scan

(For this activity, contact your local supermarket, and let the manager know you'll be coming in with your group to investigate products and types of advertising. Bring along paper and a pencil for each person.)

Walk or drive the kids to the nearest supermarket. Give each person a piece of paper and a pencil. Have kids walk through the store and list product advertisements and packaging that draw attention away from other similar products. Encourage kids to list all the items that appeal to them because of their advertising and packaging.

After about ten minutes, return to your classroom, and have kids tell about their findings. Then ask:

● **What causes people to buy certain products?**

● **How were you influenced by the packaging of the items you listed?**

● **How does the world package beliefs and philosophies so people will follow them?**

● **How easy is it to follow Jesus when the world's advertising is so much "flashier"?**

Say: **Following Jesus isn't easy when the world constantly advertises other "gods" and tells us why we should follow them. Today we're going to explore how to follow Jesus even when everyone else says, "Follow me."**

❏ Option 2: Calling All Dogs

(For this activity, arrange for a friendly dog to visit your class at the start of your lesson time. You'll need some dog treats.)

Have kids sit in a large circle. Explain that you've invited a friend to join you today. Then give two or three kids dog treats, and let the dog into the room. It's likely the dog will visit everyone at first before choosing to become "buddies" with the kids holding the dog treats.

Have kids see if they can get the dog's attention away from the people holding the treats. Then, after a few minutes, have the kids with the treats feed them to the dog. After the dog has eaten the treats, have the dog's owner come and get the dog. Ask the following questions (try to get at least three answers to each question before moving on):

● **What did you notice about the way the dog decided where to go?**

● **How is that like or unlike the way people choose where to go in life?**

Say: **The dog chose to follow the smells it liked.** Ask:

● **What "smells" in life are hard to resist?**

Say: **People tend to follow things that appeal to them most, just as the dog did. Sometimes following Jesus doesn't seem to be the most appealing option. Today we'll explore why it's important to follow the path Jesus walks instead of the paths the world offers.**

The Bible Experience

Which Way to Follow?

(For this activity, you'll need a Bible for each group.)

Form two or three groups, and give each group a Bible. Have kids choose leaders for their groups. Then have each leader choose someone to be the reader. The rest of the group members should participate in the discussion that follows the reading.

Have kids follow their group leader around the church grounds while each reader reads 1 John 3:7-10. Have group leaders take their kids through lots of different locations (under tables, around pews, in and out of rooms, up stairs, and so on). While they're still being led around the church, have kids discuss what this passage says about following Jesus. Encourage kids to explore all aspects of the Scripture passage, including why we're to follow Jesus, what pulls people away from following Jesus,

and what Jesus does to attract people to following him. You might want to write these discussion ideas on a piece of paper for each group.

After eight to ten minutes, have kids come back to the classroom.

Ask them to discuss the following questions in their groups and then report to the whole group:

● **What was it like to be led on this unusual trek while trying to study the Scripture passage?**

● **Is following Jesus always easy? Why or why not?**

● **What does your study (and this experience) tell you about following Jesus?**

Say: **Unlike the advertising we see on television and in magazines, Jesus doesn't advertise all sorts of benefits for people who follow him. Instead, he simply commands us to follow him because it's the right thing to do. But it's not always easy to follow Jesus, especially when others stand in our way. Still, with support from each other, we can do it.**

Reflection and Application

Pair Writing

(For this activity, gather a pencil, paper, and a Bible for every two students.)

Form pairs, and give each pair a pencil, paper, and a Bible. Have partners grip the same pencil and attempt to copy 1 John 3:10 onto the paper. Tell kids they must both attempt to write the passage, not just hold onto the pencil while their partner does the work. Afterward, ask:

● **What was this experience like?**

● **What made pair writing so difficult?**

● **Whose handwriting does the writing most resemble? Explain.**

● **How is the way you struggled with each other to write the passage like the way people struggle when they try to follow Jesus and the ways of the world at the same time?**

Say: **It's impossible to follow Jesus and live your life your own way at the same time. When we choose to follow Jesus, we choose to give up our former lives and walk where Jesus walks. In other words, we let Jesus write out the story of our lives, and we walk confidently beside him.**

Have partners determine one way they can support each other's walk with Jesus in the coming week. They might choose to call each other and see how well they're "following" or meet to study the Bible together. Encourage kids to follow through on their plans.

(For either of these activities, have a favorite snack ready in a nearby room or enclosed area. Keep it hidden from the kids.)

❏ Option 1: Follow Me

(For this activity, you'll need a Bible.)

Have a volunteer read aloud Matthew 4:18-19. Ask:

● **What does this passage tell us about how Jesus leads people?**

● **How easy would it be for you to get up and follow Jesus without knowing where he'd lead you?**

Explain to kids that you're going to lead them somewhere to close your meeting. Don't tell them where you're going. When kids have lined up, lead them in a roundabout way to your snack room. Before eating the snacks, have volunteers pray, asking God to help them to be confident followers of Jesus.

❏ Option 2: Knowing, Loving, Following

Say: **In our last three lessons, we've studied the basics of Christian faith—knowing, loving, and following Jesus. And we've explored parts of 1 John to see how closely these three concepts are related.**

Have kids form trios and take turns explaining to each other what it means to know, love, and follow Jesus. Tell kids to imagine they're explaining this to a non-Christian friend. Then have volunteers tell the whole group what it was like to explain the basics of faith.

Encourage kids to boldly tell their friends about what it means to know, love, and follow Jesus. Close in prayer, then tell kids to follow you for a surprise. Lead kids to the snack room, and enjoy the snacks together.

Goal:
There's power in prayer.

Scripture Verses:
Hebrews 4:15-16

Communicating With God

Prayer often seems like an empty exercise, especially to young Christians. Prayer is simply sharing heartfelt feelings with a Friend who understands. The power of prayer comes with understanding and experience. As we learn that Jesus has been where we are, we gain confidence in prayer and increase our communication with God.

Choose Your Opening

❏ Option 1: Follow the Bouncing Prayers

(For this activity, you'll need to pin a roll of adding machine tape to the ceiling across the middle of your classroom and get two small, bouncy balls.)

Form four teams. Then have each team form a single-file line facing the center of the room—two teams on each side of the line pinned to the ceiling. Give a bouncy ball to the first person in each line on one side of the room.

Say: **The people with the bouncy balls must bounce the balls on the floor and attempt to make them hit the adding machine tape that's attached to the ceiling on the first bounce. Then the first people in the lines across from them must catch the balls and attempt to hit the adding machine tape in the same way. After someone attempts to hit the tape, that person must move to the back of his or her line. Keep track of the number of hits your team gets. The team with the most hits wins the game.**

Play until each person has had at least one attempt to hit the adding machine tape. Then have kids sit with their teams in a circle to discuss the following questions:

● What was it like to try to hit the line on the ceiling?

● How is this like or unlike the way you feel when you try to pray to God?

Then say: **Sometimes it seems that prayer is a hit-or-miss activity. But if we see prayer as a "sometimes it works, sometimes it doesn't" proposition, we lose confidence in prayer. Today we're going to build our confidence in the power of prayer.**

❏ Option 2: God's Answering Machine...Not!

(For this activity, you'll need a working telephone and an answering machine on which you've prerecorded the message "Hello, this is God. I can't answer your prayer right now because..." Set up the telephone and answering machine on a rarely used phone line in your church or at your home.)

Dial the number of your "doctored up" answering machine, and listen for the message. Then invite volunteers to call the same number to hear the message. Ask:

● **How is the message on this machine like or unlike your own prayer time?**

● **How would you complete the message on this answering machine?**

Have kids complete the answering-machine message with reasons they think they might not be heard by God. For example, someone might say, "I can't answer your prayer right now because I've got more important prayers to answer." Encourage kids to speak honestly about the feelings they have when God doesn't seem to answer their prayers.

Then say: **Sometimes it seems God doesn't hear us when we pray. When we feel this way, we lose confidence in the power of prayer. But God doesn't use an answering machine because God is always home. Today we'll see how we can build our confidence in prayer.**

The Bible Experience

Approach With Confidence

(For this activity, you'll need a Bible for each student and a few concordances.)

Have kids form a circle around you. Read aloud Hebrews 4:15-16. Say: **The Bible tells us we can approach God any time with anything and do so with confidence because Jesus understands our feelings and our weaknesses. God knows how tough it is to live in this world because he's lived here as one of us.**

▶ **Extra! Extra!**

▶ If you can't set up an
▶ answering machine
▶ at an actual number,
▶ simply record the
▶ answering-machine
▶ message and play it
▶ back for kids in order
▶ to start the activity
▶ and spark discussion.

19

Give each person a Bible. Scatter the concordances around the circle. Say: **Think of a feeling you've tried to express or would like to express in your prayers. Then we'll explore the Scriptures to see if we can find a time Jesus experienced that feeling. For example, Jesus experienced sadness when his friend Lazarus died.**

Go around the circle, and have each person name an emotion. Brainstorm with the group about a time Jesus might have felt that emotion. Then find that passage in the Bible. You might want to have kids look up the emotion words in the concordances (focusing on the Gospels) to discover passages about Jesus' feelings. Remind kids that while the Bible is a record of Jesus' ministry years on earth, it doesn't include every detail of his life. Therefore, kids may not find every emotion. Assure kids that because Jesus was fully human, he knew all the feelings and insecurities we know.

After you've gone around the circle, form groups of no more than four, and have kids discuss the following questions:

● **What surprised you about this activity?**

● **What difference does it make to know that Jesus experienced the same emotions we experience?**

● **What power is there in knowing that God knows our every thought, feeling, and deed?**

● **How can we access that power through prayer?**

Reflection and Application

String Prayers

(For this activity, place a hardbacked Bible at the center of your room, and give each student a long piece of string.)

Have kids form a circle around the Bible. Say: **We have a direct line to God through prayer. And because God became like us through Jesus, we can be assured God understands our needs, concerns, and joys. But God's answers to our prayers aren't always what we hope. Fortunately, God knows what we need. Let's put what we've learned into action by talking to God about the thoughts on our minds and the feelings we're experiencing in our lives.**

We are each going to pray, silently or out loud—that's your choice. As you are praying, come forward and place one end of your string into our Bible. Hold onto the other end as you go back and sit in the circle. After everyone has prayed, the Bible will have lots of strings in it, one held by each member of your group.

Say: **Just as we're connected to this Bible by these strings, we're all connected to God through prayer. Let's commit to building our relationships with God by talking with him often.**

❏ Option 1: Like Best Friends

(For this activity, find a wastebasket and a ball that will fit inside it.)

Place the wastebasket in the middle of the room. Give one volunteer five chances to throw a ball into the basket from fifteen feet away. Give another volunteer five chances from ten feet away. Then give a third volunteer five chances from two feet away. Ask:

● **What was the key to success in this activity?**
● **How is that like the key to success in prayer?**

Say: **Prayer may sometimes appear to be hit-or-miss, like tossing this ball. However, the closer we get to God, the more we understand that prayer works! And though we may not always receive the answers we want, growing closer to God helps us see that God is indeed listening to our prayers.**

Have kids close the meeting by telling one thing each will do to grow closer to God in the coming week.

❏ Option 2: Prayer Address-Book

(For this activity, you'll need a small address book and a pencil for each student.)

Give address books and pencils to kids, and have them write their names in the front of the address book. Say: **One of the ways we can become more confident in the power of our prayers is to think about what we want to share with God. Each of us is going to start a prayer address-book so we can keep an alphabetical record of the things we want to pray about.**

Starting with A, ask kids to say aloud subjects of prayer beginning with that letter. Move on through the alphabet until kids have listed at least one subject of prayer for almost every letter. Have the kids write these subjects in their prayer address-books. Encourage your kids to keep track of answers to prayer and to continue using their books to help them pray with more power and confidence.

▶ **Extra! Extra!**

To help your kids with their devotional reading and prayer, assign them a different event in Jesus' life to read about every week. Have kids record the events (and their reactions to them) in notebooks as if they were Jesus' best friends. Every month or two, meet with individuals or small groups to hear kids' insights and learn how their prayer lives are going.

Trusting God

Preteen kids ask tough questions. Their budding ability to think abstractly challenges the simple truths they accepted as young children. The black and white of life becomes gray. Some of life seems unfair, cruel, and unexplainable. Why would a loving God allow such bad things to happen?

Kids need help to deal with the disappointment and hurt they feel when life hits them in the face. God loves them and carries them through these times, but it's hard to see that when the going gets rough. Help kids understand that the pimples, pits, and lemons of life can help make us stronger people with deeper faith.

Choose Your Opening

❑ Option 1: Perfect Life

(For this activity, bring a small suitcase or duffel bag, a large sheet of newsprint, a pair of scissors, and a marker for every three people. Have a stack of magazines and tape available.)

As kids arrive, form groups of three, and give each group a suitcase or duffel bag, a sheet of newsprint, scissors, a marker, and a few magazines. Say: **Today we're taking an imaginary trip through the Land of the Perfect Life. But before we leave, we'll need to pack. Flip through your pile of magazines, and cut out words and pictures that symbolize what's essential for a perfect life. For example, you might cut out a picture of a car. Then pack your perfect-life pictures into your suitcase.**

When all the suitcases are packed, have each group choose a representative to explain the contents of its perfect-life suitcase. List the "essentials" on newsprint, and tape the newsprint to a wall.

Then say: **Your perfect life has now changed drastically. Your house is on fire, and you're able to save just five of life's essentials in your suitcase. In your groups, choose five things you'd want to** keep in your perfect life.

Have a representative from each group report on that group's choices.

❑ Option 2: I've Always Wanted to Know

(For this activity, you'll need tape, markers, a sheet of newsprint, and several index cards for every three students.)

Form groups of three. Say: **Today we're focusing on tough faith questions, those hard questions that never seem to get answered, questions such as "Why is Sally smarter than I am?" "Why did God allow that tornado?" "Why do cheaters always seem to win?" and lots of others.**

Give each group a sheet of newsprint, tape, a marker, and several index cards. Say: **On your newsprint, draw a big, fat question mark. On each index card, write one tough question you'd like answered. Begin your questions with "I wonder why..." Put a piece of rolled tape on the back of each card, and tape the cards to the question mark. Your group will end up with several questions.**

When all the groups finish, have them tape their question mark sheets to a wall. Then say: **Let's look at how God can answer some of life's tough questions.**

The Bible Experience

Pimples in Your Life

(For this activity, provide paper, a pencil, and a Bible for every three people. You'll also need newsprint, a marker, and tape.)

Form groups of three. Give each group paper, a pencil, and a Bible. Say: **Life is rough. Bad things sometimes happen to good kids. We want everything to be perfect in life, and when it's not, we sometimes blame God or think he's forgotten about us.** Ask each group to read aloud Job 1:1-3 and 13-19. Then ask:

● **If you were Job, would you be angry at God? Why or why not?**
● **Did God still love Job? Why or why not?**

Have groups read aloud Job 1:20-22 and 42:7-17. Then ask:

● **What are reasons God allows bad things to happen to good people?**

Say: **In your groups, list three reasons on paper. Some examples might be "Bad times make us stronger" or "We learn to depend on God more."**

After a few minutes, ask a representative from each group to report his or her group's reasons. List the reasons on newsprint, and tape the newsprint to a wall. Ask:

● **How did God show his love to Jesus?**

● **Did God love Jesus when he was dying on the cross? Why or why not?**

Form pairs. Have partners sit facing each other. Ask partners to verbally list things they fear. Have the partner wearing the lightest colored shirt begin, then switch after one minute.

Read aloud Romans 8:35-39. Then say: **When bad things happen to us—when there are pimples in our lives—God still loves us. He wants us to trust him even when we're afraid. Sometimes his love is the only support we have in tough times, but it's enough.**

Reflection and Application

Life's Dilemmas

(For this activity, copy and cut apart the "Tough Dilemmas" handout on page 26. You'll also need a Bible.)

Form a circle, and place the tough dilemmas face-down in the center. Say: **Many situations in life are hard to understand. They cause strong feelings in us, and we want God to answer our questions about them. Now we'll have a chance to respond to situations that could easily happen. Someone will pick a tough dilemma from this stack and read it aloud. Then we'll respond.**

Ask a volunteer to make the first choice, and allow responses to flow freely from the group, without judgment.

When everyone has had a chance to speak on the subjects, say: **We can know that, even in the toughest dilemmas, God's love is constant and unconditional. He will always be there for us.** Read Romans 8:35-39 again.

Choose Your Closing

❏ Option 1: God's Answer

(Note: Use this closing option only if you've used the "I've Always Wanted to Know" opening option. For this activity, you'll need a marker for each person.)

Have kids regroup and stand by the question mark sheets they taped to the wall during the opening. Give each person a marker. Have kids circle any questions on the sheets that were discussed during "Life's Tough Dilemmas." Have them make an X by questions they didn't talk about. Ask:

● **Is it possible to get answers to all our questions? Why or why not?**

Then say: **We may become angry with God when we can't find answers to our questions about bad things that happen to us, to our families, or to our friends. But bad things happen because people have rebelled against God and have made our world a less-than-perfect place. Sometimes no answers seem to fit our questions. However, God will give us strength to handle anything that comes our way if we choose to trust and follow him.**

Close in prayer by thanking God for the answers he gives to us each day.

❏ Option 2: When Life Gives You Lemons

(For this activity, cut some lemons into bite-sized pieces. Make sure you have a piece for each person. You'll also need a basket of whole lemons, a pitcher of lemonade, and some paper cups.)

Hold up a basket of lemons and say: **I have a treat that looks great, and I want each of you to try it.** Have each person taste a piece of lemon. Ask:

● **How do you like the treat? Explain.**
● **How is this treat like or unlike life? Explain.**

Say: **Sometimes things that look and smell really great leave a bitter taste in our mouths. We sometimes go after things that look good on the outside without trusting God to give us the very best in his time.**

Pour a cup of lemonade for each person, and give kids time to drink it. As they are finishing, ask:

● **How is this treat like what we can do with life choices? Explain.**

Then say: **When life gives you lemons, allow God to make them into lemonade. He is faithful! In his time and in his way, all things will work together for good.**

TOUGH DILEMMAS

Photocopy this handout, cut apart the situations,
and place them in the center of the room.

1/22/98
used

- Your best friend is killed in an auto accident caused by a drunk driver. The person who caused the accident walks away without a scrape.

  What are your feelings? What do you want to ask God?

- You're eating lunch with a person who other kids think is a dweeb. A couple of people walk by and make fun of you.

  What are your feelings? What do you want to ask God?

- Your parents tell you they're getting a divorce. Your dad is moving out of the house tomorrow morning.

  What are your feelings? What do you want to ask God?

- The person sitting next to you in history cheats on a test and gets an A. You studied hard, but you get a C.

  What are your feelings? What do you want to ask God?

- Your dad is phased out of his job so a younger person in the company can be promoted.

  What are your feelings? What do you want to ask God?

- You have a terrible fight with your parents. They ground you for a month.

  What are your feelings? What do you want to ask God?

- You're walking with a group of friends, and you pass a person in a wheelchair. She doesn't have any legs.

  What are your feelings? What do you want to ask God?

- You have a broken relationship with a friend. You keep praying for God to fix it. Nothing happens.

  What are your feelings? What do you want to ask God?

- You look in the mirror and see yourself as ugly.

  What are your feelings? What do you want to ask God?

- Your grandmother is gravely ill with cancer. You keep praying for God to work a miracle and make her well. She dies.

  What are your feelings? What do you want to ask God?

- A friend says she believes people who listen to rock music are condemned by God.

  What are your feelings? What do you want to ask God?

- The TV news shows thousands of people dying of starvation in a Third World country.

  What are your feelings? What do you want to ask God?

- You discover that someone at school has started a vicious lie about you. A friend asks you if it's true.

  What are your feelings? What do you want to ask God?

Faith Sharing

Goal:
Speak out for Jesus!

Scripture Verses:
John 1:40-42;
Acts 4:18-20; and
1 John 5:7

It's easy for preteen kids to act like Christians when they're around Christian friends. But acting like Christians around non-Christians is another story.

This lesson will examine how difficult it is to talk about Jesus and will help kids experience ways to share faith naturally. It will also help them to see faith as an important element of their everyday lives.

Choose Your Opening

❏ Option 1: What's Your Commercial?

(For this activity, provide pencils, paper, and a stick of gum for each person.)

Have each person tell about his or her favorite TV commercial. Ask:
- **Why do companies advertise?**
- **What's good about advertising? What's bad?**
- **What are some things you "advertise"?**

Say: **We all advertise. For example, a guy who's really into football talks about football. That's his "commercial."**

Give kids pencils and paper. Tell them to each write down one thing they talk about often—their personal commercial. Have one student sit in front of the group while the rest of the group takes turns guessing what his or her commercial would be, based on what he or she talks about with friends. The person sitting in the front can only answer "yes" or "no" to the group's guesses. Give a piece of gum to each person who guesses correctly. Repeat the game until everyone's had a turn. Then ask:
- **Why do you talk about the topic written on your paper?**
- **Do you ever talk about your faith? Why or why not?**
- **What makes talking about your faith different from talking about anything else?**

Say: **We talk about what we like and what's important to us. Today we'll discover how we can talk about our faith just as we talk about other things that are important to us.**

❏ Option 2: Blind Without God

(For this activity, you'll need a blindfold and a card saying, "You can take off your blindfold" for each person. You'll also need a Bible. Stack all chairs against the wall.)

As kids enter the room, blindfold each one and tell them to find chairs and sit in a circle. After kids are seated, hand each student a card that says, "You can take off your blindfold." If anyone takes off his or her blindfold and peeks at the card, motion him or her to be quiet. Now read aloud 1 John 1:5-7. Ask:

● **Why are you still wearing your blindfolds?**

● **Why didn't the card help you?**

● **How was your experience with the blindfold like the experience of people who haven't heard about God?**

● **How are God and the Bible like light?**

Say: **People who don't have a relationship with Jesus need to hear about him. If God is really as important as we say, then we should talk about him.**

The Bible Experience

Tell My Brother

(For this activity, you'll need Bibles, markers, pencils, and paper for everyone.)

Say: **If something is important to us, we tell others about it. Let's look at a story about a man who told his brother something important.** Give kids Bibles, and have them form pairs and read John 1:40-42 together. Ask:

● **Why do you think Andrew told his brother about Jesus?**

Say: **Let's imagine that Andrew is a new Christian at your school. Simon is his best friend, and Andrew is anxious to tell Simon about Jesus.**

Distribute paper, pencils, and markers, and have each pair draw a cartoon illustrating this conversation. Kids can use word balloons and put Andrew and Simon's conversation in modern language. Ask several pairs to share their cartoons. Then ask:

● **How many Christian kids at your school would say what Andrew said in your cartoon?**

● **Why is it hard for kids at your school to tell others about their faith?**

Say: **When we're excited about something, we want to share it with others. Andrew was excited about his new friend Jesus. As** we get to know Jesus better, our excitement will grow, and we can share as Andrew did.

Reflection and Application

I Swear to Tell the Truth

(For this activity, you'll need a Bible for every four people.)

Have kids form groups of four. Say: **I'm going to ask a series of questions. Each person in your group should answer each question, but you each have only fifteen seconds to respond. Try not to think about it too hard; just say the first answer you think of.** Allow one minute after each statement for groups to respond. Ask the following questions:

- **What's one reason you believe in God?**
- **What's one thing you're thankful to God for?**
- **When have you felt close to God?**
- **Name one fact you know about God.**
- **Name one person you're praying for.**
- **What's one thing God doesn't want you to do?**
- **How can a person know God?**
- **How has God shown you he loves you?**

Have someone in each group read aloud Acts 4:18-20. Then ask:

- **What have you seen and heard about God that was easy to talk about in your group? What was difficult?**

Say: **Talking about what you've seen or heard about God is sharing your faith.**

Choose Your Closing

❑ Option 1: In God We Trust

(For this activity, be sure to have a penny for each person.)

Give each person a penny. Form pairs. Ask everyone to find "In God We Trust" stamped on the coin. Have partners tell each other what they think these words mean. Challenge kids to give that penny to a friend at school and talk with that friend about what "In God We Trust" means.

Close with a prayer, asking God to help kids be willing to share their knowledge of Jesus with others.

❑ Option 2: Without Being Weird

(For this activity, you'll need a chalkboard and chalk or a large sheet of newsprint and a marker.)

Fact:

The world has always thought Christians were a little fanatical about their faith. Paul, one of the greatest witnesses for the Christian faith, was thrown into prison for more than two years and then killed for speaking about what he'd seen and heard about Jesus. And what did he do while in prison? He wrote a large portion of the New Testament!

Say: **Often we don't talk about God because we're afraid people will make fun of us. Let's try to come up with some things you could say to your friends about God that wouldn't be too weird.**

Have kids brainstorm one-liners about God that wouldn't seem weird to their friends. Some examples are: "God loves me!" "We did something really cool at church," or "I think prayer in school is a good idea." There may be disagreement on what's too weird, but let kids decide. Write the one-liners on a chalkboard or newsprint.

Close in prayer, asking God to help kids find ways to talk about Jesus with their friends.

Section 2:
Free to Be Me!

What Good Am I?

Not smart enough! Not pretty enough! Not athletic enough! Not spiritual enough!

That's what kids often hear about themselves—from parents, friends, school, the media, and sometimes even the church. And unfortunately, kids often believe the message. By the time they reach their preteen years, kids have well-formed self-concepts. And more often than not, their self-concepts are low.

Use this lesson to help kids learn what's special about each of them, discover Christlike qualities in themselves, and learn what God thinks of them as individuals.

Choose Your Opening

❏ **Option 1: Bag o' Esteem**

(For this activity, provide a marker, a large paper bag, and scissors for each person.)

Give each person a marker and a large paper bag. Supply scissors, and have kids cut holes in their bags for eyes, nose, and mouth. Have kids write their names on their bags and then put the bags over their heads.

Tell kids to walk around the room and write single words of praise, such as "awesome" or "great," on other people's bags. After a while, have kids remove their bags and read the affirmations. Ask:

● **How did you feel as you affirmed others?**

● **How did you feel as you read what others wrote on your bag?**

Say: **Today we're going to reveal some more awesome affirmations about some awesome people—you! Let's start by dressing up for the occasion.**

❏ Option 2: Bag o' Goodies

(For this activity, bag up a wide assortment of wrapped candies, and make sure there's enough for each person to have one.)

Have kids sit in a circle. Pass the bag of candy around the circle, and let each person pull out a piece of candy.

One at a time, have kids give their candy away to someone else in the circle. As they give away their candy, have them complete this statement: "You're like a (name of candy) because..." For example, someone might say, "You're like a Tootsie Roll Pop, because your smiles last a long time." Instruct kids to keep all statements positive.

If a person receives more than one piece of candy, he or she must give away all of the extra pieces (using the same affirmation process) until everyone in the room has one piece of candy.

Allow kids to eat their candy. Then ask:
● **How did it feel to hear your friends say nice things about you?**
● **Why is it important to feel good about who you are?**

Say: **Today we're going to reveal some "sweet" truths about some "sweet" people—you! Let's start by changing into something more comfortable.**

The Bible Experience

Clothed With Christ

(For this activity, collect a hefty supply of newsprint, tape, markers, and scissors. You'll also need a Bible. Don't forget to recycle the newsprint when you are finished!)

Form groups of no more than four, and give each group a supply of newsprint, tape, markers, and scissors. Read aloud Galatians 3:26-29. Say: **Let's find out what it means to be "clothed with Christ." For each person in your group, create a list of positive qualities that person has that remind you of Jesus, such as kindness and honesty.** Give the kids several minutes to work on their lists. Then say: **Now I'd like each of you to create a piece of paper clothing, such as a jacket, a pair of shoes, a hat, or a belt, to represent each of your Christlike qualities. For example, one person might make a hat and write the word "kindness" on it. Then put on your new designer clothes. Go!**

Have kids model their clothing. Give everyone a rousing round of applause. Ask:
● **How does it feel to be "clothed" in your Christlike qualities?**
● **Are you always so aware of your awesome qualities? Why or why not?**

Leader Tip

As you lead this meeting's affirmation activities, keep in mind that many preteens may not feel comfortable sharing how they feel about each other. To help kids feel secure, set up specific guidelines for each affirmation activity. For example, allow no laughing or talking while each person is sharing. Also, give kids a structure to follow, such as "You're a neat person because..."

● **Why is it sometimes hard to believe that you're special?**

Reflection and Application

Putting on the New You

(For this activity, you'll need a Bible and a marker for each person.)

Say: **Let's hear all the reasons we're special!** Have kids take turns removing their paper clothing. As each piece is removed, have the person removing the clothing say, "I am (name of the quality on the clothing)." Continue until all of the paper clothing is removed. Have kids fold each piece of their paper outfits and place the outfits in piles in front of them.

Say: **Let's hear another reason we're special. Jesus chose us to be his friends!**

Read aloud John 15:12-17. Ask:

● **What are ways we can follow Jesus' command to love each other and show others they are special?**

Ask kids to offer ways to love others, such as sending notes of encouragement or being friendly to everyone at school. Give everyone a marker, and have each person write on a piece of paper clothing one way he or she will show love to another person this next week. Have kids share their ideas.

Say: **In God's eyes, each of you is special and infinitely valuable. Jesus chose each one of you to be his friend. Let's remember to follow Jesus' command and show love to others. Take your paper clothing home to remind you of your Christlike qualities and to remind you to reach out in love this next week.**

Choose Your Closing

❏ Option 1: Our Awesome Mural

(For this activity, you'll need newsprint, tape, a marker for each person, a cassette or CD of upbeat background music, and a cassette or CD player.)

Tape a sheet of newsprint to the wall. Give each person a marker. Have kids write their names creatively on the newsprint, leaving an open space beneath each name.

Play upbeat background music while kids write positive statements about each person under his or her name. Tell kids to keep the statements short and to focus on inner qualities rather than outer appearances. For example, someone may write, "You have a great sense of humor!" rather than "You're so cute!"

When everyone is finished, have kids read what others wrote about them. Post the newsprint for several weeks to remind kids of how special

Extra! Extra!

Ask kids to think of creative ideas for building one another up. List the ideas on newsprint. Then complete at least one affirmation every week!

they are. Close your session in prayer, thanking God for making your kids such awesome creations.

❏ Option 2: Appreciation Epidemic

Form huddles of no more than four kids. In each huddle, have kids each tell the person on the right one positive reason they appreciate that person. For example, someone might say, "I appreciate you because you always tell me the truth."

When everyone is finished, say: **Each of you does many special things that others appreciate. But you're worthy to be loved just because Jesus says so. And that's good enough for me!**

Close with prayer, then have kids give themselves a rousing round of applause.

Let's Talk About Love

F aith, hope, and love are all integral aspects of being in a relationship with God and with other people. The greatest of these is love, which should be at the heart of all we do. Help kids discover how important faith, hope, and love are to them.

Choose Your Opening

❏ Option 1: Trading for Love

(For this activity, prepare three placards, each with one of the following words written on it: "Faith," "Hope," and "Love." Hide the placards under three upside-down boxes.)

Select two kids to play Let's Make a Deal. Ask the contestants to jointly choose a box. After the contestants reveal the word under the box, have the rest of the group describe what the contestants have won (that is, define the word). Then ask if the contestants want to keep their prize or trade it for another box. If they trade, give the first prize to two other kids and have the first contestants choose one of the remaining boxes. Continue until all three placards have been revealed and defined by the group.

Form groups of no more than four to discuss the following questions:

● **Which prize do you believe is most valuable? Why?**

● **Which of these prizes do you value most in your relationships with others?**

● **What are the roles of faith, hope, and love in relationships?**

Say: **Today we're going to explore why each of these three qualities is important and why love is the most important of all.**

❏ Option 2: Hymnbook Love Look

(For this activity, collect paper, pencils, and a hymnal for every three students.)

Form groups of no more than three, and give each group a hymnal, paper, and pencils. Say: **Use the next five minutes to go through the hymnal and define the words "faith," "hope," and "love" using only what you find in hymn lyrics. For example, you might find a hymn that defines faith as "trusting God." See how many definitions you can find for each word, and list them on your paper.**

After five minutes, call time. Have volunteers from each group tell about their findings. Choose one familiar hymn that was used to define one of the words, and have kids sing it together. Then ask:

● **Which word was most difficult to define using the hymns? Which was easiest?**

● **Why are there so many songs about love?**

● **Which of the three characteristics—faith, hope, or love—is most important in your life?**

● **Why does the Bible give top priority to love?**

Say: **Today we're going to explore faith, hope, and love, and we'll see why love always comes out on top.**

The Bible Experience

Love: Apply Within

(For this activity, collect or create generic employment applications, pencils, and Bibles.)

Give each student a pencil and an employment application. Say: **We're going to complete these applications to fill the job openings for "love," "faith," and "hope." Imagine that you're completing this application as one of these three characteristics. Fill out the sections as you imagine love, faith, or hope might complete them. For example, in the "name" space, you might list other names love might go by. Or in the "address" section, you might describe where faith is found. Or you might list things hope is most known for in the "experience" section. Choose one of the three words (without telling anyone else your choice), and complete the application.**

Allow enough time for kids to fill out the applications. Then call time, and form groups of no more than four (make sure each group includes at least one person who filled out the application as love). Then have kids tell what they stated on the forms. Ask someone in each group to read aloud 1 Corinthians 13:4-8. Ask:

● What do these applications tell you about faith, hope, and love?

● What does the Scripture passage add to your definitions of love?

● Why is love so important in your relationship with God? with others?

● What happens when you have faith but not love? hope but not love?

● What makes love the most important characteristic of all?

Reflection and Application

Penny Graph

(For this activity, you'll need thirty pennies for each student.)

Have kids sit on the floor, as far away from each other as possible. Give each person thirty pennies. Say: **Use your pennies to make a graph illustrating how well you're doing with each of the three characteristics—faith, hope, and love. No one else needs to see your graph, and you don't need to tell anyone which of the three columns is which. But you must use all of the pennies. making a longer line of pennies for the area you're doing best in and a shorter one for the area you need to work on. Begin by making a graph of how much love, faith, and hope you have in your current relationship with God.**

Give kids a couple of minutes to make their graphs, then say: **Think about your graph and what it tells you about your relationship with God. Then move the pennies around, if necessary, to show what you'd like your graph to look like.**

Allow time to move the pennies. Now say: **It's important to have all three characteristics of faith, hope, and love in our lives. But the Bible tells us that love is the most important of all, and it explains what true love is all about. Let's express that kind of love to one another as our closing.**

Choose Your Closing

❑ Option 1: A Penny for Your Thoughts

(For this activity, give each student a handful of pennies.)

Have each person walk around the room and give a penny and a "loving thought" to at least three other people. Explain that the loving thoughts must be personal, honest expressions of love toward the other people. For example, someone might say, "I give you this penny of love because you've been a great example of love in my life" or "I give you this penny because I really care about you."

When kids have finished trading pennies, close by having volunteers ask God to help them seek more faith, hope, and love in their relationships with God and with others.

❏ Option 2: A Penny Message

(For this activity, give each student a handful of pennies.)

Have kids go around the room and silently express their love for one another in creative ways using pennies. For example, someone might approach a member of the group and spell out the word "love" using his or her pennies. Or another might simply give the pennies (and a hug) to someone else.

Give kids a few minutes to express their love, then have everyone work together on a "picture of ultimate love" by organizing the pennies on a table into a large cross-shape. Have volunteers close by thanking God for showing us what love is all about through the life, death, and resurrection of Jesus.

Goal:
God gives real-life blessings!

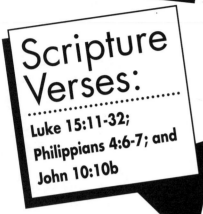

Scripture Verses:
Luke 15:11-32;
Philippians 4:6-7; and
John 10:10b

Fantasy or Fact?

As preteen kids develop the ability to think idealistically, they tend to trade in reality for fantasy. "If only I had a different family…" or "If only I were the top athlete and most popular person in school…then life would be wonderful." The "if only" of life blinds us to God's real blessings. This lesson will take a look at how God's love helps us on the road back to realistic expectations.

Choose Your Opening

❏ Option 1: Shipwrecked

(For this activity, obtain two life jackets if possible. If life jackets are not available, use two coats. Designate one side of your room as a sinking ship, and place the life jackets or coats there.)

Have all the kids stand by the life jackets on the "sinking ship" side of your room. Tell them that the other side of the room is Fantasy Island. Say: **Your ship is sinking fast. The lifeboat has been destroyed, but you do have two life jackets. Each life jacket can support the weight of one and a half people. You need to get everyone safely off the sinking ship and to Fantasy Island. Whoever is wearing a life jacket can "swim" by walking between the ship and the island, but anyone not wearing a life jacket must be carried. You choose who wears the life jackets. Good luck!**

When all the kids have landed on Fantasy Island, congratulate them on their successful escape. Then ask:

● **What was easy or hard about escaping your sinking ship?**
● **What problems do people try to escape from in real life?**
● **How do fantasies help people escape their problems?**

Now say: **Often when people face problems, stress, or bore-**

dom, they use fantasy—wishes or daydreams—to help them escape. They fantasize that life would be better if only they had more money or a bigger house or a better anything. Today we'll see that God's real-life blessings are better than any fantasies.

❑ Option 2: Finding Facts

(For this activity, you'll need a box of toothpicks.)

Form groups of no more than four, and have each group sit in a circle. Give each person five toothpicks. Say: **Think of one fact people don't know about you; for example, someone might say, "I can run ten miles without stopping." Also make up one fantasy about yourself, but make it believable; for example, someone might say, "I have traveled in Mexico." One at a time, tell your fact and fantasy, then have the rest of your group guess which is the fantasy. Everyone who guesses wrong must give you a toothpick, but you must give a toothpick to everyone who guesses right.**

When all groups have finished, ask:

● **Who in your group had the most believable fantasy?**

● **Why do we use fantasies to escape our problems or boredom in life?**

Then say: **Sometimes people use fantasies—wishes or daydreams—to escape from life's problems, stress, or boredom. Today we'll see how God's real-life blessings are better than any fantasy.**

The Bible Experience

Son on the Run

(For this activity, provide a grocery sack and markers for each person. You'll also need a Bible.)

Give each person a grocery sack and a marker. Tell kids to draw a face and a thought balloon on their sacks. In their thought balloons, have kids write a common fantasy people their age might have, such as being the most popular person in school or magically acquiring fame and fortune. Have kids show their completed sacks to the group.

Ask kids to put their sacks over their heads and walk until they touch a wall. Then have them take off their sacks and sit down in a circle. Ask:

● **What are some common fantasies?**

● **How did it feel to try to "see through" your fantasy?**

● **How is that like or unlike trying to see through our fantasies in real life?**

● **How can our fantasies blind us to what's going on around us?**

Then say: **Sometimes we get lost in our fantasies about how life**

would be so much better "if only" we had more wealth or more friends or nicer clothes. Our fantasies may blind us to some good things God has already given us. Let's hear a Bible story about a son and his fantasies.

Read aloud Luke 15:11-19. Form two groups. Give each group another grocery sack and a marker. Instruct both groups to draw the son's face and a thought balloon on their sacks. Have one group write in its thought balloon the son's fantasy. For example, this group might write: "Fortune! I'll have the time of my life!" Have the other group write in its thought balloon the son's thoughts about what really happened. For example, this group might write: "Living with pigs! I'd be better off at home."

Have both groups present their sacks. Ask:
- **What were the son's fantasies?**
- **How were his fantasies different from reality?**
- **When have you been disappointed by a fantasy that didn't come true?**

Then say: **Let's read more about what happened to the son when he returned home.**

Reflection and Application

Road to Reality

(For this activity, you'll need index cards, pencils, and a Bible.)

Read Luke 15:20-32 aloud. Ask:
- **What blessings awaited the son when he came back to reality?**
- **How is fantasy different from reality?**

Give each person an index card and a pencil. Have kids write on one side of their cards one problem they're facing at home or school. On the other side of their cards, have them write good things God has given them right now, such as friends, food, home, and health. Ask:
- **How can the blessings you've listed help you handle the problem you're facing?**
- **How are the blessings you've listed better than the fantasies you dream about?**

Choose Your Closing

❏ Option 1: Full Life

(For this activity, you'll need the cards from "Road to Reality," a big bag of popped popcorn, and a Bible.)

Form a circle, and have kids join hands. Say: **Let's pray for what we've written on our cards.** Have kids pray silently about what they've written on their own cards. Close by reading aloud Philippians 4:6-7. Then say: **Sometimes people use fantasy to escape their problems. Sometimes they want more excitement than they think real life has to offer. But listen to what Jesus promises.**

Read John 10:10b aloud. Stand in the center of the circle with the bag of popcorn, and invite kids to hold out their hands. Approach each student, and fill his or her hands so full of popcorn that they overflow. As you do this, say to each student: **Jesus came so you could have life— life in all its fullness.**

❏ Option 2: Fantastic Facts

(For this activity, you'll need the cards from "Road to Reality," additional index cards, pencils, and a Bible.)

Form a circle, and have kids join hands. Say: **Let's pray for what we've written on our cards.** Have kids pray silently about what they've written on their own cards. Close the prayer by reading aloud Philippians 4:6-7. Then read aloud John 10:10b, and say: **When you know Jesus, your real life can be better than any fantasy.**

Give each person an index card and a pencil. Have kids each write a short, real-life affirmation of the person on their right. For example, someone may write, "You are a good friend" or "You are fun to be around."

Have kids exchange cards. Tell kids to save the cards as reminders that real life is better than any fantasy.

Fantasy or Fact?

▶ **Extra! Extra!**

If you have time, have kids customize Luke 15:11-32 to fit their home situations. Have them include their fantasies about a better life and their current, real-life blessings.

Goal:

Parents are grrreat people!

Scripture Verses:

Ephesians 6:1-4; 1 Corinthians 13:4-7; and Romans 5:1-2

"I Love You" to Parents

Preteen kids are often so self-absorbed that they appear to be hibernating—cut off from the outside world. They may neglect to show their true feelings, especially at home. They want to be involved in family life, yet their peers are becoming ever more important because they "understand." Moving from child to teen is a big step, and it is often hard to tell which side of the line the emerging preteen student is standing on.

Use this lesson to help kids express their feelings about family life.

Choose Your Opening

❑ Option 1: Lap Leap

(For this activity, arrange chairs in a circle—one chair for each person.)

Have kids sit in the chairs. Say: **Today we'll focus on parents. Sometimes it's hard to tell your parents you love them. The words get stuck! Even though you do love them, it's hard to show it. During this lesson, we'll have a chance to think and talk about our parents' good points.**

I'm going to read statements that may or may not reflect things that happened to you during this past week. If a statement is true for you, move in the direction I indicate. If it's not true for you, stay seated. If someone is in the seat you're supposed to move to, sit on that person's lap. Read these Lap-Leap Statements aloud:

1. **Move one seat to your right if you said "I love you" to your parents.**

2. **Move two seats to your left if you had an argument with your parents.**

3. **Move one seat to your left if you fought with your parents about the bathroom.**

4. **Move one seat to your left if you were told to clean your room.**

5. **Move three seats to your left if you helped with the dishes.**

6. **Move four seats to your left if you were grounded.**

7. **Move one seat to your right if you yelled at your parents.**

8. **Move two seats to your right if you talked about school problems with your parents.**

9. **Move five seats to your left if you talked with your parents privately.**

10. **Move one seat to your right if you helped cook a meal.**

11. **Move three seats to your right if you slammed your bedroom door.**

12. **Move four seats to your right if you lied to your parents.**

13. **Move three seats to your left if you felt your parents were always too busy for you.**

14. **Move two seats to your right if you argued with your parents about the telephone.**

15. **Move four seats to your left if you talked with your parents about a problem.**

16. **Move five seats to your left if you cried with your parents.**

17. **Move one seat to your right if you had family devotions together.**

18. **Move four seats to your right if you had a heated discussion with your parents about the music you listen to.**

After you've said the last Lap-Leap Statement, ask:

● **What did you learn about how you relate to your parents?**

● **Do you feel that you have a generally good or bad relationship with your parents? Explain.**

Read aloud Ephesians 6:1-4. Ask:

● **Does this Scripture passage describe what goes on at your home? Why or why not?**

❑ Option 2: Best Vacation

(For this activity, you'll need an index card, a sheet of paper, and a pencil for each student.)

Give each student an index card, a sheet of paper, and a pencil. Say: **It's easy to think about the bad aspects of living with our parents. But it's important to think of the good times we've shared with them as well. On your index card, write a description of the best vacation or weekend outing you've ever had with your family. Don't go into great detail; just write the basics. You may write something like this: "We went camping together. It rained. The tents leaked. We got soaked. It was a mess. But we sure had fun." Don't write your name on the card.**

Collect the cards, mix them up, and hand them back to the kids. Make sure no one has his or her own card. Then have each person read aloud the card he or she was given. After each card is read, have kids each guess whose vacation it was by secretly writing a name on their papers. After all the cards are read, have kids reveal whose experience is whose.

After the game, ask:

● **What was special about all the family adventures we just heard about?**

● **Do you think the best is yet to come with your parents? Why or why not?**

The Bible Experience

Family-Love Review

(For this activity, you'll need a "Family-Love Review" handout and a pencil for each person. You'll also need a Bible, and you'll need to make a row of ten chairs.)

Give each person a "Family-Love Review" handout and a pencil.

Say: **The love statements on this Family-Love Review are taken from 1 Corinthians 13:4-7.**

Read aloud 1 Corinthians 13:4-7. Say: **In these verses, the Apostle Paul is talking about the meaning of Christian love. Read each statement on your handout, and rate yourself—from one to ten— on each love quality. Be fair and truthful.**

Point out the ten chairs in a row, representing the family-love ratings from one to ten. Then read aloud each statement in the Family-Love Review, and have each person stand by the chair that represents the number he or she circled on the review for that statement. Ask:

● **Why is it hard to show real love to your parents?**

● **In what area did you rate yourself lowest? highest?**

● **What are some things you can do to raise your lower ratings?**

Reflection and Application

Parent Brag-Line

(For this activity, you'll need a ball of twine, tape or tacks, markers, and plenty of construction paper and clothespins.)

Tape or tack the twine across the room from wall to wall in several places. Place the construction paper, clothespins, and markers on a table in the center of the room. Ask:

● **What makes you proud of your parents?**

● **What are some big and little things they do to make you feel special?**

● **Has your dad made a special effort to do something with you? When?**

● **Has your mom been there to support you during a tough time? When?**

Say: **On the construction paper, write the ending to this statement: "I'm proud of my mom or dad because . . ." Write as many different responses as you can think of, each on a separate sheet of paper.**

Have kids use clothespins to hang the sheets of paper on the twine. Then have kids walk around and read the responses. Gather in a circle. Ask:

● **What did you learn about yourself as you started thinking about things your parents do that you're proud of?**

● **Why is it sometimes hard to brag about your parents?**

Choose Your Closing

❑ Option 1: Letters to Parents

(For this activity, you'll need a "Love Letter to My Parents" handout, a pencil, and a stamped envelope for each person.)

Give each person a "Love Letter to My Parents" handout and a pencil. Say: **It's easier to brag about your parents when they can't hear what you say. But they need to know how much you care about them. Complete this love letter to your parents. No one but your parents will see what you write.** When the kids have finished, ask:

● **Can one person talk about something you've written in your letter?**

● **How was this difficult for you? easy?**

● **What effect will this letter have on your parents?**

Give each person a stamped envelope. Have kids put their letters in the envelopes and seal and address them. Walk as a group to the nearest mailbox to let kids mail their letters, or gather them to mail yourself. Another option would be to save the stamps and have kids hand deliver the letters to parents after the church service.

❑ Option 2: God's Grace

(For this activity, you'll need a Bible.)

Form a circle, and read aloud Romans 5:1-2. Talk about the fact that God's grace is a gift of love. Then have kids join hands, and ask each person to complete this sentence: "Today I learned . . ."

Close with a prayer thanking God for parents.

Family-Love Review

Read each of the "Love is..." statements. Then rate yourself from one to ten on how much you share that quality of love with your parents with one meaning "never" and ten meaning "always."

1. Love Is Patient

I'm patient with my parents. I try to see their side of issues and understand their motives.

NEVER 1 2 3 4 5 6 7 8 9 10 ALWAYS

2. Love Is Kind

I'm thoughtful and caring toward my parents. I try to build them up. I appreciate what they do for me, and I let them know it.

NEVER 1 2 3 4 5 6 7 8 9 10 ALWAYS

3. Love Does Not Envy

I don't get upset when my parents do something I don't get to do. I don't keep a running score on what they get and then demand my equal share.

NEVER 1 2 3 4 5 6 7 8 9 10 ALWAYS

4. Love Does Not Boast

I don't try to be the most important person in my family. I don't want excess attention. I work to help my parents feel important.

NEVER 1 2 3 4 5 6 7 8 9 10 ALWAYS

5. Love Is Not Proud

I don't think I'm better than my parents. I don't put my parents down when they don't measure up to my expectations.

NEVER 1 2 3 4 5 6 7 8 9 10 ALWAYS

6. Love Is Not Rude

I don't mouth off to my parents. I don't deliberately hurt my parents with my actions or language.

NEVER 1 2 3 4 5 6 7 8 9 10 ALWAYS

7. Love Is Not Self-Seeking

I don't try to make my parents conform to my way of doing things. I don't demand my own way just to make things easier for me.

NEVER 1 2 3 4 5 6 7 8 9 10 ALWAYS

8. Love Is Not Easily Angered

I don't blow up at my parents when I don't get my way. I don't intentionally irritate my parents.

NEVER 1 2 3 4 5 6 7 8 9 10 ALWAYS

9. Love Does Not Remember Wrongs

I forgive my parents. I don't hold grudges against them, and I don't make fun of their mistakes.

NEVER 1 2 3 4 5 6 7 8 9 10 ALWAYS

10. Love Rejoices in Truth, Not Evil

I don't laugh at my parent's failures. I appreciate my parents' honesty with me even when the words are not what I want to hear.

NEVER 1 2 3 4 5 6 7 8 9 10 ALWAYS

11. Love Does Not Give Up

When I become angry with my parents, I don't give up on our relationship. I keep trying to work out our disagreements.

NEVER 1 2 3 4 5 6 7 8 9 10 ALWAYS

Love Letter to My Parents

Dear_____,

   Sometimes it's so hard to share my feelings with you. I'm just going through so many changes inside, and I don't always know what to say. I hope this letter helps.
   I love you. I probably don't say that enough.
   I really appreciate the way you_____
_____
   I remember a time you_____
_____
and I never told you how much that meant to me.
   I appreciate how patient you've been about _____
_____
   I never told you how much I admire you for _____
_____
   I wish we could _____
_____
   I think it would help our relationship.
   I guess our biggest struggle right now is over _____
_____
Can we spend time talking about it?
Faith is important to me, but I keep wondering about
_____
   I want you to know that I'm glad you're my parents. You're the best.

Love,

Section 3:
Forever Friends

Goal:
....
To have good friends,
be one!

Scripture Verses:
....
Matthew 16:13-23

Making Friends!

Friends are important to preteen kids. As they begin to spend more time with friends than with family members, kids discover they really want friends they can depend on. However, they often lack the skills to develop lasting friendships.

This lesson will help kids learn how to develop friendships that are deep and lasting. Kids will discuss the importance of lasting friendships and look at Jesus and his friendship with his disciples.

Choose Your Opening
....

❏ **Option 1: Wearing It**

(For this activity, use a permanent marker to write "Real Friends Always . . ." on a large, white T-shirt. You'll also need several other permanent markers.)

When kids arrive, give each person a permanent marker, and have them take turns writing their completions for the sentence by writing on the T-shirt. Make sure everyone adds at least one sentence completion. Duplicate ideas are OK.

Have a male volunteer put on the T-shirt, and have kids sit in a circle around the T-shirt wearer. Ask another volunteer to read aloud the sentence completions. Then ask:

● **Which sentence completions describe the most important qualities of a real friend?**

● **How easy is it to find friends who have these qualities?**

● **What qualities do you wish you'd see more of in the friends you have?**

Say: **Real friendship isn't easy. It takes commitment, honesty,**

52

and love. Lots of people are looking for real friends. Today we'll discover how to be a real friend.

❏ Option 2: Grab a Group of Friends

Welcome kids as they arrive, and explain that they'll play a simple game to start the lesson. When you call out a number, kids must quickly huddle together in a group consisting of that number of friends. For example, if you yell "five," kids should group together in fives. Kids who don't get into groups fast enough are out for that round. Play a few rounds of the game, randomly yelling numbers from two through nine.

Then form one more set of groups (of no more than four each, with everyone participating), and have kids discuss the following questions in their groups:
- **What was it like to huddle together with friends in this activity?**
- **How did it feel when you got into a group? when you didn't get into a group?**
- **How is this like or unlike the way you feel when you're trying to make friends with people in real life?**

Say: **This game is a lot like real life—friends often come and go, and sometimes it's not easy to make friends. But it's possible to build lasting relationships. Today we'll explore how.**

The Bible Experience

Friendship Can Sting

(For this activity, you'll need a chenille wire for each group member and a Bible.)

Begin by asking:
- **What kind of friend do you think Jesus is?**

Have kids call out their answers. Then explain that you'll be looking at a story about Jesus and Peter, one of Jesus' closest friends.

Give each person a chenille wire. Say: **As I read aloud Matthew 16:13-20, listen for ways Jesus showed real friendship to Peter. When you hear something that shows how Jesus lived out real friendship, form your chenille wire into a shape that represents that idea. For example, if you think Jesus affirmed Peter, you could shape your chenille wire into a heart.**

Read the passage a second time while kids look for good examples of Jesus' true friendship. Here are some ideas: Jesus affirmed Peter, Jesus showed confidence in Peter, Jesus showed that he trusted Peter, and Jesus shared his own ministry with Peter.

Have kids explain their chenille-wire shapes to the whole group. Then read Matthew 16:21-23 twice while kids shape their chenille wires into representations of Jesus' true friendship as recorded in this passage. Here are some ideas: Jesus shared personal concerns with Peter, Jesus was painfully honest with Peter, Jesus spoke the truth to Peter, and Jesus wouldn't let his friends come between him and God.

Then have kids trade chenille-wire shapes and attempt to explain the shapes to the whole group. After a few volunteers have explained the shapes they're holding, have the original owners explain what the shapes symbolize. Ask:

● **What was it like to explain someone else's chenille-wire shape?**

● **How is that like the way you felt when looking for examples of friendship in the second passage?**

● **How easy was it to find examples of friendship in this passage?**

● **What surprises you most about Jesus' actions in this passage?**

Say: **Being a real friend means speaking the truth—even when it hurts. To be forever friends, we need to be willing to speak the truth in love and to be honest with one another. And we need to be willing to listen to the truth spoken by our friends.**

Reflection and Application

Still Shots

(For this activity, provide an instant-print camera and film, poster board, and a marker.)

Have kids call out the ways Jesus showed friendship to Peter as you list them on the poster board. Then have kids identify the four or five most important qualities of a true friend, and circle them.

Form groups of no more than four. Assign one of the circled friendship qualities to each group. Ask each group to imagine what a photograph would look like that could show how people express friendship using that assigned quality.

Then have kids pose for their pictures while you take instant-print photographs of them. Have kids attach the photos to the poster-board list as a visual reminder of what it takes to become forever friends.

Choose Your Closing

❏ Option 1: Flex Your Friendship

(For this activity, you'll need index cards and pencils, a cassette or CD player, and a cassette or CD with one of the songs listed on page 55.)

Extra! Extra!

Instead of using an instant-print camera, use a video camera to videotape kids acting out scenes showing modern-day applications of the ways Jesus expressed friendship. If you don't have access to an instant-print camera or a video camera, have kids create human sculptures representing the friendship qualities Jesus expressed.

Give each person an index card and a pencil. Have kids write the name of a friend across the top of their cards. Encourage kids to choose someone who means a lot to them and who they hope will be a forever friend.

Play one of the following songs: "Friends" or "For You" by Michael W. Smith (from the album *Go West Young Man*) or "A Friend Like You" by Geoff Moore (from the album *A Friend Like You*). While the song is playing, have kids list at least three ways they could build their friendships with the people listed at the top of their cards. Encourage kids to list ideas based on what they've learned about Jesus' friendship style.

Close by having kids pray silently that God would help them be real friends to the people on their cards and to all of their friends.

❏ Option 2: Hold Onto That Friend

Form a circle, and have everyone stand close together facing the inside of the circle. If you have more than ten kids in your group, form multiple circles of no more than ten people each.

Have each person reach his or her right hand into the center of the circle and grab someone else's right hand. Then have each person reach his or her left hand into the circle and grab a different person's left hand.

Say: **Friendship is something worth holding onto. It's not always easy to build lasting friendships, but it's worth the effort.**

Have kids attempt to untangle themselves to form a larger circle without letting go of their two friends' hands. Then have volunteers close in prayer, thanking God for the gift of friendship.

Goal:
Face conflict as God's child!

Scripture Verses:
Matthew 5:21-26, 38-48; Romans 12:14-21; and 1 John 4:17-21

How to Fight Right

For many preteen kids, the schoolyard is like "the valley of the shadow of death." Why? That's where bullies do their bullying. Experts estimate that up to five million American kids are either bullies or victims of bullies.

Why do kids handle conflict by bullying others? Their sense of justice is simply stronger than their sense of mercy. They look for black-and-white, instant solutions to their problems. But unconditional love is Jesus' style of conflict resolution. To him, the only good fight is the fight for love. Use this lesson to challenge kids to respond to conflict God's way.

Choose Your Opening

❏ Option 1: Tollbooth Bully

Stand outside your meeting-room door. As kids arrive, tell them each to give you a quarter. If they don't have a quarter or won't give you one, make them stand outside of the room.

When all the kids have arrived and are either inside or outside of the room, allow the kids standing outside to enter the room. Ask:

● **How did you feel when I demanded a quarter before you could enter the room?**

● **Why did you respond as you did?**

● **How was this experience like being bullied in real life?**

Say: **Since the beginning of time, there have been people who love to bully others into giving them what they want. Although we often hear about how we're supposed to "stand up" to bullies, there are some dangers involved in doing so. Let's learn biblical ways to deal with bullies.**

Give kids their quarters back!

Fact:
The number of kids arrested for violent crimes increased by 48 percent in the five years between 1985 and 1990.

❏ Option 2: Feeding the Fish

(For this activity, you'll need a large bowl of popped popcorn.)

Place the bowl of popcorn on a table. Tell kids to pretend the room is a giant fish-tank with three kinds of fish in it. Choose two kids to be the Freshwater Sharks. Then form one group to be the Whining Darters and one group, twice as large as the Whining Darter group, to be the Groupers. Have each group choose an area in the room to be its nest.

Say: **I'm going to feed the fish in my fish tank. When I say, "Let's eat," all of you should act true to your identities. Groupers, you are cautious fish, so each of you should come to the table, take five pieces of food, and carry them to your nest before coming back to get five more pieces. Whining Darters, you don't know anything about gathering your own food, so you depend on other fish to feed you. All you can do is come to the table and beg other fish to feed you. When someone gives you food, take it to your nest and then come back and beg for more. Freshwater Sharks, you are aggressive. You get your food by taking it from other fish. If you approach any of these other fish and demand their food, they must give it to you. You then must take your newly acquired food to your nest before demanding more food from others. Ready? Let's eat!**

After five minutes, call time, and ask:

● **How do you feel about the role you and others played in this activity?**

● **How are the roles some people played like real-life bullies?**

● **How did you deal with the bullies in this activity?**

● **How do you deal with bullies in real life?**

Say: **Today we're going to talk about biblical ways to deal with bullies.**

The Bible Experience

Bully Busters

(For this activity, provide Bibles, paper, and pencils.)

Form four groups. Give each group a Bible, some paper, and a pencil. Say: **Each group is a bully-busting task force that helps people deal with bullies. I'll give your group one Bible passage to read. Your task force should list one thing people should do to deal with bullies and one thing people should not do, according to your passage. Choose a recorder to write your ideas on paper. Then choose a task force reporter to share your findings with the large group.**

Assign each group one of these passages: Matthew 5:21-26; Matthew 5:38-48; Romans 12:14-21; and 1 John 4:17-21.

Have reporters share their findings. For example, reporters may say things such as "People should make peace with bullies," "Don't fight back, let God punish them," "Wish good for them," or "Don't hate them."

Then ask:

● **Why does God tell us these ways to deal with bullies?**

● **What biblical advice is easiest for you to follow? most difficult? Explain.**

Say: **God has given you these guidelines for dealing with bullies. God has also given you caring adults to help you, such as teachers, pastors, parents, and youth leaders. If you need help handling a tough situation, feel free to ask advice from any of these people who care about you.**

Reflection and Application

Give and Take

Form pairs of kids of approximately the same size and weight. Say: **Partners, stand shoulder-to-shoulder, facing in opposite directions, so that your left feet and left shoulders are together. Now reach out, and lock left hands with your partner. When I say "go," try to push or pull your partner off-balance so that his or her right foot moves. We'll try this three times to see who does the best. Ready? Go!**

After three tries, call time, and say: **Now think of the biblical ways to deal with bullies. Let's try this activity again, only this time, respond in a God-honoring way.**

See how kids respond. They might let a partner win, talk out a compromise, or put an arm around another and say, "I wish you the best." Then ask:

● **How did you feel as you were doing this activity the first three times?**

● **How did responding in a biblical way make you feel?**

● **Which response felt the best? Explain.**

Say: **We often respond to bullying by getting tough with the other person, which can make matters worse. Biblical responses can bring peace in conflicts.**

Choose Your Closing

❏ Option 1: The Bully in Me

(For this activity, you'll need newsprint and markers.)

Form pairs, and give each pair a sheet of newsprint and a marker. Have pairs draw a human "bully" shape on their newsprint. Say: **Before we can do anything constructive about the bullies in our lives, we must admit that there are times we bully other people. Partners, tell each other one time you bullied someone, such as a time you threatened a younger brother or sister so you could get your own way. Write the situations on your newsprint.**

After pairs have finished writing, have them place their newsprint bullies in the center of the room. As a large group, join hands in a circle around the newsprint bullies. Pray: **God, please forgive us for bullying others. Help us respond in a Christian way to those who bully us. Amen.**

❏ Option 2: Let's Talk

Have kids form pairs. Have partners tell each other about one bully they have trouble with (they don't have to use names) and one response they'll use to deal with him or her. Then have partners name one person they have bullied (such as a younger brother or sister) and say one way they'll change their behavior.

Close with a prayer, asking for God's strength and help in dealing with bullies.

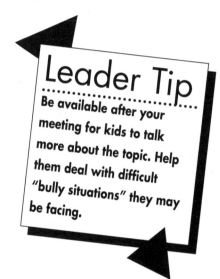

Leader Tip

Be available after your meeting for kids to talk more about the topic. Help them deal with difficult "bully situations" they may be facing.

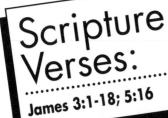

Goal:
Lift each other up!

Scripture Verses:
James 3:1-18; 5:16

Encouraging Words

Kids endure daily put-downs from classmates and others at school and in their neighborhoods. To defend themselves, they return fire with their own put-downs. Words can be damaging to young and old alike.

The tongue—such a small organ—can control, hurt, demand, share, console, restore, and love. In this lesson, kids will learn ways to choose words to help, not hurt.

Choose Your Opening

❏ Option 1: Like a Fire

(For this activity, provide a large sheet of newsprint, markers, matches, and a Bible. Find a safe place outside to place a metal trash-can or barrel in which you can burn the newsprint.)

Take kids outside, near the metal trash-can. Have kids form a circle around the newsprint. Have someone read aloud James 3:3-6. Have kids shout words or phrases that can "burn like fire" when used against others. These could be names such as "Four Eyes" or "Brace Face," or put-downs such as "You're so stupid." List these words or phrases on the newsprint. Ask:

● **How can these words influence your life when they are used about you?**

● **What happens to your friendships when you use these kinds of words in times of anger or haste?**

● **How can this be compared to a forest fire? Explain.**

Hold the newsprint by one corner over the metal container. Say: **Words can burn, even when they're said in jest or as a joke. They can cause irreparable damage in a matter of seconds.** Have some-

one light the bottom corner of the newsprint with a match. When the fire is burning well, but before it endangers your hands or clothing, lower it into the metal container, and drop it. Remain silent while the paper finishes burning. Then ask:

● **Can we put this paper back together to remove the words from it?**

● **How is this like or unlike words spoken in anger to family or friends? Explain.**

Say: **Today we're going to look at ways to use our tongues to encourage and bring peace rather than to hurt and anger.**

❏ Option 2: Big Damage

(For this activity, fill two clear pitchers with water. You'll also need a box of cornstarch; a packet of sweetened, dry, fruit-flavored drink mix; one large spoon; and small cups.)

Hold up one pitcher of water, and ask: **Who is willing to take a drink?** Have kids raise their hands. Drop a spoonful of cornstarch into the water, and stir it up. Ask again who would be willing to take a drink. Repeat this process with the other pitcher but, instead of cornstarch, drop the fruit-flavored drink mix into this pitcher and stir. Then ask:

● **What difference did what I added make in your desire to drink the water from the first pitcher? from the second?**

● **How is this like or unlike words you "drop" at times when you are talking to people?**

Say: **Cornstarch isn't a bad thing, but it made the water unpleasant to drink. The fruit-flavored drink mix made the water in the second pitcher seem more drinkable. It sure made it colorful!**

The Bible tells us about a very little thing that can be used for good or can cause a lot of damage. Today we're going to be looking at how important it is to control it. I'm talking about your tongue.

Serve some fruit drink to anyone who wants it.

The Bible Experience

Big Difference

(For this activity, you'll need a sheet of paper, a pencil, and a craft stick for each person. Have a Bible and a large basin of water ready.)

Have each person make a paper boat from a sheet of paper using the diagram in the margin. Have kids write their names on their boats and open the bottom of the boats slightly so they will stand up. Give everyone a chance to float their boats and blow them across the water in the basin.

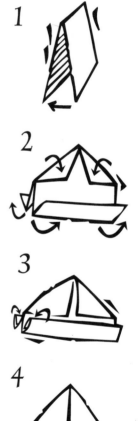

Now give each person a craft stick. Have kids make rudders by inserting their sticks into the bottom of their boats along the angle of the triangle in the middle so the stick protrudes about an inch from the bottom of the boat. Have kids test their boats again by blowing them across the water. Then set the boats aside to dry, and ask:

● **What was it like when you tried to blow your boat across the water the first time? the second time?**

● **What made the difference?**

Read aloud James 3:3-5. Ask:

● **How is your tongue like the rudder you put on your boat?**

● **How does your tongue affect what you do?**

● **How does your tongue help you? hurt you?**

● **How does your tongue sometimes hurt other people?**

Reflection and Application

Damage Control

(For this activity, you'll need Bibles, pencils, and paper.)

Have kids form groups of four. In each group, have kids appoint a reader, someone to summarize their discussion, a recorder to take notes, and a reporter to recap their discussion for the whole class.

Say: **Your group is an immigration inspection committee. The tongue has just applied for permanent entry into your country. You must decide if it is too great a risk to allow the tongue into your country. First read aloud James 3:3-10. Make a list of damaging things the tongue does. Include in your list damaging things mentioned in the passage and things you know from personal experience. Then decide whether the tongue should be admitted to your country.**

Give groups about five minutes to complete their lists and make their decisions, then have them report to the class. Ask:

● **Without mentioning names, how has someone's tongue hurt you?**

● **How have you hurt others with your tongue?**

● **What kinds of things should we avoid saying with our tongues?**

Then say: **In your groups, read again James 3:8-10. Review your list of damaging things, and decide how we could make a conscious effort to change the way we use our tongues. See how many of these damaging things your group can turn into encouraging ideas.** After four or five minutes, have reporters share their groups' thoughts on encouraging words.

Say: **Tongues are more powerful than most of us realize! They can** do terrible damage, but with God's grace and our own conscious efforts, we can use our tongues to encourage and help others.

Choose Your Closing

❏ Option 1: The Good Side

(For this activity, provide a Bible, a chalkboard and chalk or newsprint and a marker, and a box or several bars of Bit-O-Honey candy.)

Have kids remain in their groups of four. Say: **Another part of James tells us about things we can do to use our tongues in a positive way.** Read aloud James 5:16. Ask:

● **What good uses for the tongue does this passage suggest?**
● **What are some words you can say to encourage others?**

List kids' suggestions on a chalkboard or newsprint. Hand each person several pieces of Bit-O-Honey candy, then say: **In your groups, each person can choose one of these good words and use it to encourage another member of your group. As you give encouragement, sweet words from the tongue, to another person, give that person a Bit-O-Honey.**

Give kids a couple of minutes to encourage one another, then have them remain in their groups and close in prayer for one another.

❏ Option 2: Tongue Stoppers

(For this activity, you'll need the boats from the "Big Difference" activity and pencils.)

Have kids retrieve the boats they made earlier. Give each person a pencil. Say: **We all have a tendency to use words in hurtful ways. We listed some of those ways earlier. On the inside of your boat, write a note asking God to help you deal with one way you've been using words to hurt rather than to encourage or heal.**

Have kids form pairs, and have partners share with each other what they've written on the inside of their boats. Then have each person suggest specific ways his or her partner can use what he or she has written to encourage others. Have partners encourage each other to follow through on their commitments. Tell the kids to keep their boats as a reminder that their tongues are like the rudder that guides a big ship— with big consequences!

Close in prayer, thanking God for helping us to control our tongues and to give encouragement.

Goal:
The word is out—
Respect!

Scripture Verses:
Romans 12:10 and
1 Peter 3:8-12

Respecting Others

Preteen kids struggle to know how to relate to others. In the unsure process of fumbling for identity, many kids focus on their own needs and brush aside what it means to show respect for others. Today's lesson will look at what the Bible says about respect. Kids will discover ways to show respect to parents, peers, neglected people, and authority.

Choose Your Opening

❏ Option 1: Disrespect

(For this activity, provide balloons, markers, and a pin.)

Welcome kids, and give each person a balloon and a marker. Have kids inflate and tie off their balloons. Say: **Think of a person you'd like to say unkind things about, and draw that person's face on your balloon. Choose someone you don't respect, but don't let anyone know who your picture represents.**

When kids have finished, say: **Call out disrespectful things to your balloon faces, as if you're talking to the people the balloons represent. Don't say actual names, and don't use bad language. For example, you could yell: "You don't know a thing. Why should I listen to you?"**

After about thirty seconds, walk around the room and begin popping the balloons with the pin. Pop as many balloons as possible before kids try to prevent them being popped.

Then gather kids in a circle, and ask:

● **How did you feel when you were showing disrespect to your balloons?**

● **How is this like or unlike the way people show disrespect toward others in life?**

- **Why do we disrespect others?**
- **What was it like when your balloon was popped?**
- **How is what happened to the balloon like what happens when we show disrespect to people?**

Say: **Today we'll explore how Jesus showed respect to others. We'll learn how we can also be respectful.**

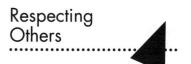

❏ Option 2: Respect Yourself

(For this activity, bring a cassette or CD player and a recording of songs about respect. Check local record stores or libraries for songs such as "R. E. S. P. E. C. T." by Aretha Franklin.)

Form a circle. Play a song about respect, then have kids stand and demonstrate the song's message through an action or words directed at a person across from them. For example, kids might greet each other with kind words.

After playing all the songs, ask:
- **What do these songs say about respect?**
- **Why is respect important in relationships?**

Say: **Respect is something we know about but probably don't frequently practice. It's too easy to say unkind or disrespectful things to people we don't like. But today we'll discover through Jesus' example that it's important to respect others.**

The Bible Experience

Respecting Others

(For this activity, provide newsprint, tape, markers, and Bibles.)

Tape a sheet of newsprint to a wall, and title it "Respect." Have kids call out definitions for the word "respect," and list these ideas on the newsprint. Then have someone read aloud Romans 12:10 and 1 Peter 3:8-12. Have kids amend their definitions in light of these verses.

Form four groups, and give each group a sheet of newsprint, a marker, and a Bible. Assign each group one of the following topics and related Scripture passages:
- respecting parents (Ephesians 6:1-3; Proverbs 13:1)
- respecting peers (Matthew 20:25-28; 1 John 4:19-21)
- respecting neglected people (Matthew 18:1-4; John 4:7-10)
- respecting authorities (Leviticus 19:3; Hebrews 13:17)

Say: **Read your Scripture passages, discuss what they say about your topic, and list on the newsprint ways to show respect to your assigned group. For example, the group assigned "respecting peers" might write, "Don't think of yourself more**

"highly than others" based on the insights the group gleaned from Matthew 20:25-28.

After five minutes, have volunteers present their groups' ideas to the class. Then ask:

● **What do these passages teach you about respect?**

● **Why is respect seldom demonstrated in our society?**

● **Why is it important to show respect to one another?**

Say: **Showing disrespect to others is a game we shouldn't play. Let's take a few moments to practice respecting one another.**

Reflection and Application

I Respect You

Say: **Respect comes easily when we like a person. But it's a lot harder to respect someone when we disagree with that person or dislike what he or she does.**

Have kids form groups of about four. Tell groups to choose a topic members might disagree on, such as the death penalty, helping the poor, politics, movie ratings, hiding the truth from parents, or the importance of homework or grades. After group members have found a topic they disagree on, have them discuss the topic while showing respect for one another through words or actions. Say: **Remember, you don't need to agree with other people to show them love and honor. For example, you could listen to another person's opinions without interrupting, then say, "That's an interesting point of view" before offering your own opinion.**

After about five minutes, ask:

● **How easy or hard was it to show respect while disagreeing? Explain.**

● **What lessons did you learn about showing respect to others?**

Say: **It's not always easy to show respect to others. But with Jesus' help, we can be kind and courteous to one another even when we don't agree or get along.**

Choose Your Closing

❏ Option 1: Paying Respects

Have kids form a row. Say: **Let's close by showing the respect we have for each other.**

Have the first person walk along the row, greeting and shaking hands with each person in line until he or she joins the line at the other end. Repeat this process until each person has respectfully greeted the entire group.

Then have volunteers close in prayer, thanking God for the Bible's guidance on respecting others.

❏ Option 2: My Commitment

(For this activity, you'll need paper, envelopes, pencils, and stamps.)

Give each person a sheet of paper, an envelope, and a pencil. Say: **Think of someone you've been disrespectful toward. This could be a friend, parent, or even God. Then write a short letter to that person, asking for forgiveness for your actions. When you've written your letter, address it so it's ready to mail.**

When kids finish their letters, have them decide if they want to mail them or talk to the person they've written to. If kids have written letters to God, suggest they spend time this week in prayer, asking for forgiveness. If kids decide they want to mail their letters to friends or parents, supply stamps for them to do so.

Have kids join hands as you close in prayer, asking for God's help in showing respect to others.

▶ **Extra! Extra!**

After the meeting, host a "Respect Yourself" party. Play the songs about respect, serve snacks, and play affirmation games. For example, have kids affirm each other by saying, "One thing I really respect about you is . . ."

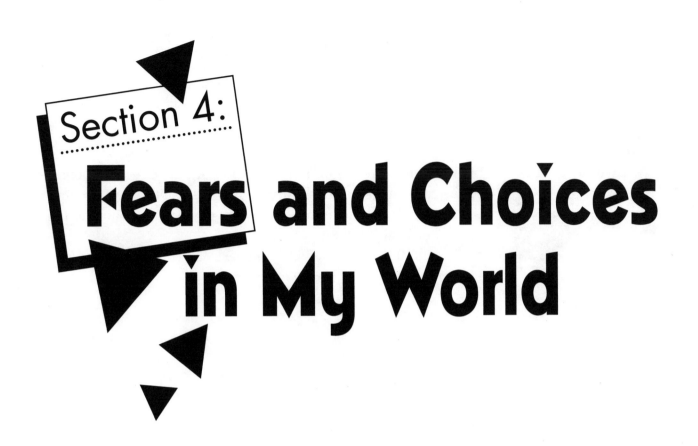

Section 4:
Fears and Choices in My World

Goal:
Unmask the evils around us!

Scripture Verses:
**Ephesians 6:10-18;
John 10:10; and
Romans 16:17-20**

Everyday Evils

Evil. The word conjures up all kinds of images—scary, ominous, satanic images of dark forces. But evil isn't always so obvious. Preteen kids encounter evil every day—things such as hurtful words or dishonest actions.

Through this lesson, kids will unmask the subtle evil they face and discover that not all evil is easy to recognize.

(For this lesson, place four pieces of poster board on the wall with the word "evil" written on them, one letter on each board. These boards will stay up until the end of the lesson.)

Choose Your Opening

❏ Option 1: Masks

(For this activity, you'll need paper, markers, a bag, and a simple mask resembling a human face.)

Pass out paper and markers to everyone in the group. Give kids five minutes to draw the scariest masks they can. When they're done, have each person hold his or her mask up in front of his or her face, and have the rest of the group rate it on the "scary scale" from one (wouldn't hurt a flea) to ten (really scary). Ask:

● **What makes some masks look more evil?**

● **Are the features out of proportion?**

Have each person make another mask with another piece of paper. This time the masks should be very friendly. Rate the masks in the same way. Ask:

● **Which mask looks the most harmless? Why?**

Finish by taking a mask out of a bag. The mask should be a straightforward human face, without scars or extra eyes! Put the mask in front of your face, and ask:

● **Is my face scary or friendly?** (It should be neither!)

● **Could a mask like this hide someone terrible behind it? Why or why not?**

Say: **Today we're going to look at evil and ways to identify it in our lives.**

❏ Option 2: Everyday News

(For this activity, you'll need newspapers, poster board, glue, and scissors.)

Form groups of three, and give each group a piece of poster board, scissors, glue, and newspapers. Tell kids to cut out articles or pictures about evil people or events. Let kids determine the definition of evil as they do this. Have the kids glue the articles and pictures to the poster board. When groups have finished, have members of each group explain the pictures and articles they chose and tell why they chose as they did. Then ask:

● **Were the examples easy to choose?**
● **How would you define evil?**

Have each group write its definitions on the poster board and then tape the boards on the wall near the word "evil." Then say: **Today we're going to look at evil and how we can identify it in our lives.**

The Bible Experience

Evil Comes in All Sizes

(For this activity, you'll need a copy of the "Evil Comes in All Sizes" rap and a Bible.)

Have two kids read aloud the "Evil Comes in All Sizes" rap below. Have them wear "rapper" accessories, such as backward caps, baggy pants, or neck scarves, and have them change their voices accordingly.

Evil Comes in All Sizes

READER 1: A long time ago and far away, a man of God had this to say,

READER 2: "Put on God's armor—his sword and shield—so you can stand against what the devil wields."

READER 1: Yo friends, brothers, sisters, all. Watch out for those who want to make you fall. Stay away—don't go near. You'll be OK 'cause it's God you fear.

READER 2: For we don't fight against flesh and blood but against darkness, blackness, and evil in the 'hood.

READER 1: For these dudes aren't serving our God; they're serving themselves, deceiving everyone.

READER 2: So put on God's armor—you won't be sorry. You'll stand against evil without a worry.

READER 1: If you do what God says, I'll be full of joy. Be smart about good and dumb about bad.

READER 2: Stand firm, stand firm. And wear his armor.

READER 1: And the God of peace will crush the evil one flat. *(Stomps feet.)*

Have kids get into groups of four. Ask:

● **How were the two readers' passages different?**

● **Is some evil bigger and easier to recognize?**

● **What are some examples of that kind of evil?**

● **What are some examples of smaller, harder-to-recognize evil?**

● **Have any of you ever experienced a "bigger evil"? Explain.**

Say: **Think of a time someone hurt you by talking behind your back or disappointing you.**

● **Could this be thought of as evil? Why or why not?**

Say: **The Apostle Paul experienced this type of evil.** Have someone read aloud Romans 16:17-20. Ask:

● **What does it mean to be "wise about what is good"? "innocent about what is evil"?**

Reflection and Application

The Evil in Ourselves

(For this activity, you'll need an envelope and a pencil for each person.)

Give kids envelopes and pencils, and have them address the envelopes to themselves. Say: **You should expect to receive a letter from me in the coming week containing a Bible verse and a couple of questions for you to answer. Someone else will receive the same Scripture, and that person will be your secret partner. You'll find out who your secret partner is next week. Think about the Scripture and be ready to discuss it with your partner. Then answer the questions truthfully.**

Choose Scriptures from the following list: Psalm 37:8; Proverbs 26:23; 29:6; Isaiah 5:20; Matthew 7:11; 12:35-37; 15:16-19; Romans 2:8-11; 1 Corinthians 14:20; 1 Timothy 6:10; and 3 John 11. Assign "partners" by making sure two kids get the same Scripture. The questions should be:

- What are the five most common "evils" you see in yourself?
- How can Jesus help you remove those evils?

Mail the letters in time for them to arrive before the next scheduled meeting time.

Choose Your Closing

❏ Option 1: From Evil to Life

(For this activity, you'll need a Bible.)

Ask for four volunteers. Tell kids to rearrange the letters in the word "evil" (using the poster-board signs) so they spell something more positive. (They may spell "vile" before they spell "live," so be ready to laugh with them!) When they've spelled "live," read aloud John 10:10. Then ask:

- **What does it mean to have "life in all its fullness"?**
- **How can Jesus help you have an abundant life?**
- **Is it possible to truly live without Jesus?**

❏ Option 2: Thank You, God

(For this activity, you'll need a Bible.)

Read aloud John 10:10. Say: **Stand next to one of the letters in the word "evil." Choose a letter that begins another word having to do with life; for example, someone might choose E for everlasting life with Jesus or L for the love Jesus gives us in our lives.** After kids have moved, have them say their words and tell what the words have to do with life.

Close in a time of "popcorn" prayer—you'll start a sentence and then kids will finish it with one-word answers. Say: **God, help us as we struggle with the following evils in our lives...** Then say: **Thank you, God, that you can help us overcome evil in ourselves because you are...**

Leader Tip

At the beginning of the next meeting, have kids find their partners by finding the person who has the same Scripture as they do. Have pairs discuss their verses and name ways they think God can help them remove the evils from their lives.

Leader Tip

It's easier for kids to identify evil in others than in themselves. Don't let them focus just on everybody else—help them point the finger at themselves as well.

Goal:
Take remote control!

Scripture Verses:
2 Samuel 15:1-6;
Proverbs 8:10-11; and
Colossians 3:1-6

Media Madness, MTV, and Me

Let's face it, our kids watch a lot of television. But do they ever think about the impact it has on their hearts and minds? Preteen kids need to learn how to monitor their TV viewing habits in light of their relationships with God.

Use this lesson to discuss the influence of the media on kids' lives and to help them evaluate their favorite TV shows. Students will compare the values of Scripture with the values of the media, and they'll be challenged to commit to becoming more selective TV viewers.

Choose Your Opening

❑ Option 1: Magazine Madness

(For this activity, you'll need magazines, scissors, newsprint, tape, and markers.)

Form four groups. Give each group a stack of magazines, a pair of scissors, a sheet of newsprint, tape, and markers. Say: **Using your supplies, make a poster advertising a new TV show called "Media Madness, MTV, and Me." This show is about the members of a family whose entire lives are controlled by whatever they see on television. For example, if they see a diaper commercial, they'll immediately go to the store and buy some diapers—even if they don't have babies. Along with your poster advertising the show, create an idea for what a sample plot might include. Pick any celebrities you want to star in your show. You have five minutes. Ready? Go.**

After five minutes, have groups share their posters. Ask:

● **Why did you choose the celebrities you did?**

● **How would you feel if you were starring in this show? Explain.**

● **How is this TV show like or unlike real life?**

Say: **Life may not be like this TV show, but the truth is that television has a powerful influence on our lives. Today we're going to talk about letting God be the director of our lives.**

❑ Option 2: Imagination

(For this activity, you'll need paper and pencils.)

Form groups of no more than five. Give each group a sheet of paper and a pencil. Say: **Imagine you're a parent. What rules about television viewing would you make for your children? In your groups, write your rules on your paper.**

Have groups read their lists aloud. Then ask:

● **How are these rules like or unlike your own parents' rules?**

Say: **It's tough being a parent and having to compete with the appeal of television. Today we're going to talk about decisions that we need to make about watching television. We may learn that direction from parents and from God will change the way we let TV influence our lives.**

The Bible Experience
••

Looks Aren't Everything

(For this activity, you'll need snacks, two identical crowns, and a Bible.)

Choose two outgoing volunteers for this activity—one to play the role of King David and the other to play Absalom. It's OK if kids aren't familiar with the story (they will be by the end of the activity). Put identical crowns on the two volunteers' heads, and give Absalom the snacks. Have the volunteers stand on opposite sides of the room, and have the rest of the kids stand in the middle.

Say: **Your job is to figure out which one of these people is Absalom and which one is David, and then you'll need to side with one of them. Your only guide is what you may already know about Absalom and David. You will learn more about these two in a few minutes. Once you've decided which side to stand on, you can't change your mind. You are free to help Absalom or David gain followers.**

Pull the volunteers aside, and say: **During the game, David can only say, "God chose me to be the king"; Absalom can compliment kids, make promises, and even give out snacks. Be persuasive!**

▶ **Extra! Extra!**

As a group, watch episodes of two TV shows—such as an episode of *Home Improvement* and an episode of *Roseanne*. Then ask each person to write a one-sentence description of what each show teaches. Or post movie ads and TV Guide pages on the walls, and have group members walk around the room and look at them. Then discuss what they teach.

After five minutes, stop the game, and count who has the most followers. Ask the group:

● **How did you feel during the game?**

● **What's similar about these feelings and the feelings you have when you're choosing what to watch on television?**

Have a volunteer read aloud 2 Samuel 15:1-6. Then ask:

● **What was Absalom trying to do?**

● **What was his motive?**

● **How is Absalom's influence similar to the influence of television in our lives?**

● **How can television draw us away from God?**

Say: **Absalom deceived the people of Israel using charm, flattery, and eloquent words. He stole their hearts from King David. Like Absalom, television is full of deceptive messages. We may see lifestyles on television that look appealing on the surface, but we don't always see the real-life consequences of those lifestyles. God loves us so much, and he wants the best for us. That's why it's important for us to evaluate our TV viewing habits in light of God's instructions.**

Reflection and Application

Television on Trial

(For this activity, provide newsprint, markers, paper, pencils, and Bibles.)

Say: **We're going to put some of the most popular TV shows on trial and evaluate them from God's perspective.** Form groups of four or five people, and tell kids to call out their favorite TV shows. Write their responses on newsprint. Have the group vote on the top four or five shows, then assign one show to each group.

Distribute a sheet of paper, a pencil, and a Bible to each group. Say: **On your paper, list the positive and negative messages your show promotes. Compare your messages with Colossians 3:1-6, and discuss how your show compares with the Bible's standards.**

When the groups are ready, have them explain their findings. After each report, call for a show of hands to determine who thinks the show is worth watching and who doesn't. Ask:

● **How did you feel about evaluating a show that you like?**

● **Do you think it's important to evaluate the shows we watch? Why or why not?**

● **How can you apply this form of evaluation to all the shows you watch regularly?**

Say: **It's important to evaluate the shows we watch and become** more selective TV viewers. As we've seen in this activity, the Bible is a great guide to help us watch shows that are better for our lives.

Choose Your Closing

❏ Option 1: Hasta la Vista, Baby

(For this activity, you'll need index cards, pencils, and Bibles.)

Give each person an index card, a pencil, and a Bible. Say: **Read Proverbs 8:10-11. Then write on your card one change you'll make in your TV viewing, based on what the passage says. Make your answer specific and measurable.**

Form pairs, and have partners share their answers with each other. When pairs are finished, say: **Pray with each other, and ask God to give you the strength to keep the commitments you've made. When you get home, post your card in a place where you'll see it often, so you'll be reminded of your goal.**

❏ Option 2: Media and Me

(For this activity, you'll need a copy of the "Media and Me" handout [p. 78] and a pencil for each person.)

Say: **It's not enough to know what we should do when the media bombards us with wrong messages. God also expects us to act on what we know.**

Give each person a "Media and Me" handout and a pencil. Have kids complete their handouts.

Have kids post their completed handouts in their rooms or near their TV sets to remind them to follow through and change the channel or turn off the TV when they are tempted.

Take time now to pray with the kids. Ask God to give kids discernment in choosing which TV shows and movies to watch and which magazines to read. Ask for God's help in resisting temptation.

MEDIA & ME

Decide how the media tempts you to follow wrong teachings. For example, immoral activities seen while watching soap operas may influence your own ideas of right and wrong. Write or illustrate the temptation on the "thumb down." Then choose one way you can resist that temptation. (For example, you could turn off the television.) Write or illustrate your way of resisting that temptation on the "thumb up."

Choices—Just Say Yes to God!

Goal:

Help! God is in control.

Scripture Verses:

Psalm 145: 14-21;
John 16:31-33; and
Romans 8:31-39

Kids flip through TV channels and find people "drinking to forget" or escaping from painful situations by diving headfirst into drug use. Certainly more than a few kids observe the same responses in real life, with situations such as parents escaping a bad day at work through alcohol use.

According to a researcher at Carnegie Mellon University in Pittsburgh, kids often lack the critical information they need to make informed decisions about risky behavior.

Use this lesson to help kids discover why people drink and take drugs to escape. Kids will examine biblical ways to cope with problems and learn how God can help people in need.

Choose Your Opening

❑ Option 1: Eating Away Problems

(For this activity, you'll need snacks, newsprint, a marker, and masking tape.)

Set up the snacks on a table on one side of the room. Gather kids on the opposite side of the room from the snack table. Say: **Today we're going to discuss how some people abuse drugs or alcohol when they are faced with difficult problems. To begin, I'd like you to call out problems that are difficult to deal with.**

List the problems on newsprint, then tape the newsprint to the wall near the snack table. Say: **One at a time, I'd like you to walk up to the table, read the list until you find one problem you've faced or are facing, then eat one snack item, such as one potato chip or one grape. You may have only one item each time you come to the** table, and you must return to the opposite side of the room after each visit. You may come to the snack table as many times as you'd like, but you may have a snack item only after you find a problem on the list you've faced or are facing. You'll need to choose a different problem each time.

After three minutes, ask:

● **How did it feel to eat a snack after thinking about a problem?**

● **How is the way you ate something every time you thought about a problem like the way people sometimes deal with problems in real life?**

● **How is the way you ate these snacks like or unlike the way people use drugs or alcohol to cope with problems?**

Say: **Today we're going to discover how God—not drugs or alcohol—helps us cope with our problems.**

❏ Option 2: Have One

(For this activity, purchase a quantity of small candies, such as M&M's.)

Form groups of no more than four. Give one person in each group a supply of small candies. Say: **Those of you with the candies are to give them away to members of your group. But a group member may have candies only after you get him or her to say or do something for you; for example, you might have someone sing "The Alphabet Song" before you give him or her the candies.**

Remind kids to choose activities that aren't embarrassing or crude. After three minutes, ask:

● **How did you feel when you were asked to say or do something to get the candy?**

● **How is the way the person with the candy controlled you like the way drugs and alcohol control people?**

● **Why do people drink or take drugs?**

Say: **Many times people drink or take drugs because they want to escape a painful or difficult situation. Today we're going to explore a better way to deal with life's problems—trusting God.**

The Bible Experience

No Escape

(For this activity, you'll need two flashlights, a supply of newsprint, markers, and Bibles. This game works best if played in a room that can be made very dark.)

Choose two kids, and give them flashlights that are turned on. Say to the rest of the group: **The flashlight beams represent problems** you're facing. Try to avoid facing the problems by moving around the room away from the light beams. You can move only when you are saying, "Drink, drink, drink" or "Drug, drug, drug." If you get caught by a beam, freeze in your position.

Turn out the room lights, and have flashlight-holders attempt to catch other kids in their light beams. After three minutes, turn on the room lights, and ask:

● **How did you feel as you tried to escape the light?**

● **How is this like or unlike the way people try to escape problems with drugs or alcohol?**

Say: **Sometimes people abuse drugs or alcohol as they blindly try to run from their problems. But the problems don't go away.**

Form three groups. Give each group a sheet of newsprint, a marker, and a Bible. Assign each group one of these passages: Psalm 145:14-21; John 16:31-33; or Romans 8:31-39. Have groups read their passages, discuss what they say about facing difficult problems, and list their discoveries on the newsprint.

After five minutes, call time, and have a volunteer from each group share the group's discoveries. Ask:

● **How does God help us in difficult times?**

● **How is God's help different than attempting to escape our troubles through drugs or alcohol?**

● **What are ways we can trust God to help us during tough times?**

Say: **Drugs and alcohol don't make our problems go away. But God always walks with us and helps us overcome all difficulties.**

Reflection and Application

Finding Hope

(For this activity, you'll need a flashlight.)

Form a circle, and turn out the room lights. Shine the flashlight on the person across from you, and say: **God's light can help you through tough times.**

Pass the flashlight to the person on your left, and have him or her repeat the process. Continue in this manner around the circle until the flashlight is returned to you. Have kids pray silently, asking God to help them avoid drugs and drinking.

Choose Your Closing

❏ Option 1: No Problem Is Too Large

(For this activity, you'll need a balloon for each person and a pin.)

Give each person a balloon. Say: **Think about a problem you're currently facing. Then inflate your balloon to a size that represents how big that problem seems to you.**

Kids don't need to tie off their balloons, they can just hold them. Say: **Romans 8:37 says that in all things we have full victory through God's love. As I pop each balloon, remember that God can help you to overcome any problem you'll ever face.**

As you pop each balloon with the pin, say: **God is bigger than your problems.**

Then have kids help each other pick up the balloon pieces to show how we can help each other "pick up the pieces" after we go through tough times.

❏ Option 2: Banded Together

(For this activity, you'll need a Bible.)

Extra! Extra! ◀
Ask a drug-abuse counselor to attend your next class. Allow time for kids to ask more questions and receive answers.

Have kids form a tight circle. Say: **God is as near as the word "help." Rather than turning to the temporary escape of drugs or alcohol when we have problems, let's commit to seeking God's help in tough times.**

Have kids say together, "We commit to support each other in tough times and to seek God's help above all else."

Then read aloud Psalm 145:18 as a closing prayer, and have kids form a group hug.

Running the Race

Goal: Keep on keeping on!

Scripture Verses: 1 Corinthians 9:24-27

"When the going gets tough, the tough get going." At least that's how the saying goes. In reality, it's much more common for today's preteen kids to give up when things get tough—or to not try at all. That's because in today's instant-everything, immediate-gratification world, many kids don't understand the meaning of perseverance.

This lesson will let kids experience what it's like to persevere. They'll explore what the Bible teaches about perseverance and discover new ways to "run the race" of life with faith.

Choose Your Opening

❏ Option 1: Keep at It

(For this activity, you'll need to create three "determination stations." Use the suggestions below, or come up with your own ideas.

● *Video Game station—Have a video game (or two) that kids must "persevere" at in order to improve (or win).*
● *Card-Stacking station—Provide lots of playing cards.*
● *Free Throw station—Provide a basketball goal and a basketball or a trash can and a bunch of paper wads.)*

Form three groups, and have each group go to one of the stations. Say: **If you are at the Video Game station, you must attempt to get the highest score (or win the game). If you are at the Card-Stacking station, you must stack as many cards as possible into a tall "house of cards." If you are at the Free Throw station, you must try to score as many baskets in a row as possible.** Encourage everyone to work together in their groups to reach the goals of better, higher, and more.

Every four minutes, have groups change stations until everyone has visited all three stations. Then have kids form trios consisting of one member from each group. Ask:

● **What was it like to try to better your score, card-house size, or number of shots made in a row?**

● **Did you ever feel like giving up? Why or why not?**

● **How is the way you kept at this like the way you must persevere in everyday life? How is it different?**

● **What kinds of things stop us from persevering in our lives?**

Say: **Today we're going to explore how perseverance can help us when things get tough.**

❏ Option 2: One More Time...

(For this activity, you'll need a bag of rice and a bunch of black or other solid-colored plates.)

Set up tables and chairs, and form pairs. Have partners sit across from each other at a table. Then give each pair a plate and a handful of rice. Say: **I'm going to assign each pair an item to illustrate using the rice, such as a house with a dog in the yard, an airplane with clouds, or a person holding a balloon. You'll create your illustration by placing the rice, one grain at a time, onto your plate. If you pick up more than one grain of rice at a time, you'll have to start over.**

Make the suggestions difficult, yet not impossible, for kids to complete. Then have kids begin their work. After a minute or so, interrupt kids and say: **One more thing... at times, the table will shake, which might mess up your work. Be prepared.**

During the next few minutes, watch to see that kids follow your instructions. Bump or shake the table from time to time. It's OK if kids try to save their creations by picking their plates up off the table.

Allow plenty of time for kids to attempt their illustrations, then have kids show what they've done. Ask:

● **What was it like to work on this project?**

● **Did you ever feel like giving up?**

● **When have you felt like that in life?**

Say: **In our faith, as in all aspects of our life, sometimes things get tough or get in our way. Today we're going to explore how perseverance can help us get through the tough times.**

When Things Get Tough

(For this activity, you'll need Bibles, concordances, and small prizes.)

Form groups of no more than four. Give each group a Bible and a concordance. Say: **Your group must find and discuss a Scripture passage about perseverance. The passage you're looking for contains the word "race." Use your concordances to find it. If you think you've found it, show me, and I'll let you know if you're correct. You must tell me exactly which verse or verses I'm looking for in order to proceed into the next part of this activity. Each group who finds the exact passage will win prizes.**

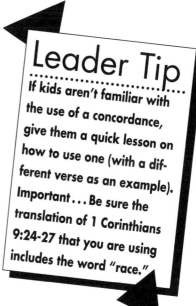

Leader Tip

If kids aren't familiar with the use of a concordance, give them a quick lesson on how to use one (with a different verse as an example). Important... Be sure the translation of 1 Corinthians 9:24-27 that you are using includes the word "race."

The passage you want your kids to find is 1 Corinthians 9:24-27. Award the prizes to groups as they find the exact passage. Have groups discuss these questions:

- **What does it mean to persevere in faith?**
- **What does Paul say about determination in this passage?**
- **Why does Paul bother to persevere in faith?**
- **What prize is Paul talking about?**
- **When has it been tough to persevere in your faith?**

After six or seven minutes, call everyone together to share insights from their discussions. Ask:

- **How was the search for the passage like the message of the passage?**
- **What happens if we "give up" when things get tough?**
- **How does God help us persevere?**
- **How has God helped you persevere in the past?**

Say: **Paul knew the importance of perseverance even in the middle of difficult times. When we run into problems or difficulties, it's often easier to give up or give in than to strive to "win the race." But we can persevere with God's help and a little encouragement from one another.**

Reflection and Application

Why Try?

(For this activity, you'll need volleyball equipment.)

Form teams for a game of volleyball. Make sure everyone gets to play at the same time (team size can vary, depending on the number of kids in your class). Then begin playing a version of volleyball where kids try to keep the ball in play for as many hits as possible (but no more than three per side). Have kids count aloud as they keep track.

After each series of hits when the group succeeds in improving on its previous best volley, pause the game, and have kids share ideas on how to persevere in their faith. Have kids think of things they can do on their own, such as pray, study the Scriptures, and go to church; and have them think of things they can do to help others, such as listening to a friend who's hurting.

Play until kids have improved their best volley at least three times. After the game's over, add your own ideas about persevering in faith.

Choose Your Closing

❑ Option 1: Running the Race

(For this activity, you'll need snacks.)

To close the lesson, have kids run a prayer relay race around your church (or other nearby building). Form teams of four, and have team members each take a turn running around the building while silently praying a prayer about perseverance.

To "hand off" the prayer to the next runner, team members must first say aloud; "Thanks for listening to my prayer. Now please listen to (name of next team member)'s prayer." The last person on a team must call out "amen" when crossing the finish line.

When everyone has run the race, celebrate and enjoy the snacks together.

❑ Option 2: Perseverance Prayer

(For this activity, you'll need snacks.)

Form a circle. Explain ahead of time that you'll be going around the circle four or more times (as many times as you think would be a bit of a challenge for kids) in a prayer about perseverance. Beginning with you, go around the circle and have everyone add to the prayer. Remind kids that they can repeat thoughts that have been spoken if they can't think of something new, but ask them to try their best to add something new to the prayer.

Suggest that kids ask for specific help with situations they're facing or thank God for times when he's helped them stay "in the race" when things were tough.

Begin the prayer by saying: **Dear God, help us persevere in faith . . .** Close the prayer with a unison amen. Enjoy the snacks together.

Section 5:
Finding My Place

Goal:
Faith shines in our actions!

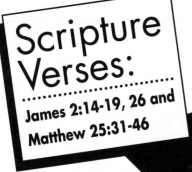

Scripture Verses:
James 2:14-19, 26 and Matthew 25:31-46

Faith Works!

Many kids today are convinced that doing good is their best shot at gaining God's favor. However, faith in Jesus is what will get them to heaven. Our good works demonstrate our faith just as Jesus demonstrated servanthood to us.

This lesson will look at the faith that brings forth action—at home, at school, and in the community. Kids will be challenged to live out their faith in the world where God places them.

Choose Your Opening

❏ Option 1: Faith to Ride

Say: **Raise your hand if you rode to church today in some sort of a motor vehicle.** Form groups of four, making sure that each group includes one student who raised a hand. Have groups discuss the following questions:

● **What kind of faith did you need to have in a vehicle in order to ride in it?**

● **How could that vehicle disappoint you?**

● **How did your actions demonstrate the faith you had in that vehicle?**

● **What could have happened if that vehicle had not lived up to your faith in it?**

Say: **Before you ride in a car, you need to have faith that it will get you safely where you want to go. Before sitting in a chair, you need to have faith that it will hold you up. Today we're going to be talking about faith and how our actions are affected by our faith.**

❏ Option 2: "Dead or Alive" Scavenger Hunt

(For this activity, you'll need plastic bags.)

Form teams of three, and give each team a plastic bag. Give teams five to ten minutes to go on a scavenger hunt, collecting both live and dead items inside and outside the church. All live items are worth three points each; all dead items are worth two points each. A team may receive points for one type of item (such as a leaf, a blade of grass, or a rock) only once. Encourage creativity!

When teams return, have them briefly display their items and tally their points. Then say: **As you've discovered, we live in a world that's full of things that are either dead or alive. Today we'll learn that our faith can be defined the same way. It's either alive or dead. How can you tell whether your faith is alive or dead? Look at what you believe and what you do. That's how you know.**

The Bible Experience

Faith Without Works?

(For this activity, provide a Bible, paper, and a pencil for every four people.)

Read aloud the following passage, adapted from James 2:14-19, 26. As you read, have volunteers briefly act out the italicized words. When you read an italicized word, point to a volunteer to act it out. Don't spend a lot of time on this. Simply read, point, and resume reading.

My brothers, if someone says he has faith, but does *nothing*, his faith is worth *nothing*. Can faith like that *save* him? A brother or sister in Christ might need *clothes* or might need *food*. And you say to him: "God be with you! I hope you *stay warm* and get *plenty to eat*." You say this, but you do not give that person *the things he needs*. Unless you *help him*, your words are worth *nothing*. It is the same with faith. If faith is *nothing*, then that faith is dead, because it is *alone*.

Someone might say, "You have *faith*, but I *do things*. Show me your faith! Your faith does *nothing*. I will show you my faith by the *things I do*." You believe there is one *God*. Good! But the *demons* believe that, too! And they *shake with fear*.

A person's body that does not have a spirit is dead. It is the same with faith. *Faith* that does *nothing* is *dead*!

Form groups of four, and give each group a Bible. Ask a volunteer to read aloud Matthew 25:31-46 and tell kids to listen carefully. Then give each group a sheet of paper and a pencil. Tell groups they each have two minutes to list human needs that fit into the categories mentioned by Jesus in the passage from Matthew. (For example, a group might list a warm home, enough food to eat, and companionship in the midst of loneliness.)

After two minutes, have groups each review their human needs lists, and ask them to pick the three most important needs. Then have them brainstorm ways they could meet those needs. For example, a need of hunger might be met by sharing a lunch with a person at school. After

three to five minutes, have small groups give summary reports to the whole group.

Reflection and Application

Faith House

(For this activity, provide paper, pencils, and a couple of boxes of envelopes.)

Form teams of two or three, and give each team paper and a pencil. Tell teams they have five minutes to list as many good works as they can think of. Examples might include helping a friend, going to church, and feeding the hungry.

After five minutes, have teams add up the total number of good works they have listed. Give each team a new piece of paper, and ask them to write the word "faith" on the paper in large letters. Then give each team one envelope for each good work they listed earlier. (If a team thought of twenty-five works, give them twenty-five envelopes).

Tell teams they have five minutes to create a house using only the envelopes given to them. Each house must be built upon the team's "faith" paper. Announce that each house will be judged on its strength. After five minutes, test each house's strength by blowing on it. Determine a winning house, then gather everyone back together. Ask:

● **How do you feel about your house? Why?**
● **What would you do differently if you could start over?**
● **How is building your faith in Christ like building your house?**
● **How does your team's house compare to your faith?**
● **If God gave you a grade for your "faith house," what grade do you think you'd get? Explain.**

Then say: **Good works are as important to your Christian life as bricks or wood are to a house. A house wouldn't be complete without walls or a roof, and faith is nothing without works to make it solid.**

Choose Your Closing

❏ Option 1: Balloon Faith

(For this activity, you'll need one balloon for each person.)

Give each person a balloon. Have kids join you in demonstrating how their faith is like a balloon and how their actions as Christians are like the air that inflates the balloon. Say: **The good things we do demonstrate how real and strong our faith is.** Have kids blow up their balloons. **Faith without good actions is dead and useless.** Have kids let the air out of their balloons.

Have kids blow up their balloons again and tie them off. Ask kids to take the balloons home as a reminder of the need to act on their faith in everyday life.

Close in prayer, asking God to give kids the power and opportunity to work on the needs they've recognized.

❏ Option 2: Action!

Form a circle. Have kids tell the person on their left one thing they want to work on to help their faith grow. When all have shared, say: **Now we're going to pray for each other and encourage each other to put our faith into action.**

Have kids pray for the person on their right, asking God to help that person especially in the one area he or she mentioned. Wrap up your session with prayer. Then conclude by saying: **Let's encourage each other as we all take action on our faith.**

Goal:
Live what you believe!

Scripture
Verses:
Exodus 20;
Deuteronomy 6; John 1;
and Revelation 2–3

Actions Talk

We are often impressed by kids' Bible knowledge and class unity on Sunday mornings or at group meetings, but what happens when kids are sitting in the school lunchroom? How do they live out their faith between classes at school or in their neighborhoods? Does faith make a difference in their conversations? Can God really change the way people act?

You can help kids identify their beliefs and understand how those beliefs fit into everyday life. Use this lesson to help kids examine how God feels about hypocrisy and to identify specific ways to live what they believe.

Choose Your Opening

❑ Option 1: Real or Fake?

(For this activity, you'll need paper and a pencil for each person. Set up four "stations," and place the following items at each station. At Station 1, you'll need a cup of brown-colored water and a cup of coffee; at Station 2, you'll need a saucer of sugar and a saucer of artificial sweetener; at Station 3, you'll need a live plant and an artificial plant; and at Station 4, you'll need a stuffed animal and a picture of a real animal. Label the items at each station either A or B.)

As kids enter, give them paper and pencils. Have them number their papers from one to four. Tell kids to walk from station to station and decide which item at each station is real—A or B. They may use all of their senses to decide. Have kids write their answers on their papers.

After kids have finished, ask:
- **How did you tell the difference between real and fake?**
- **What makes something fake?**
- **How can a Christian be fake?**
- **How can you tell whether a person's beliefs are real or fake?**

Say: **Today we'll be talking about our own beliefs and the beliefs of the church. We want to look at specific ways to live what we believe.**

❑ Option 2: I Need a Ruler

(For this activity, prepare four index cards with the following beliefs written on opposite sides of each card: 1. "Help all people" and "Don't cheat"; 2. "Obey my parents" and "Don't lie"; 3. "Respect teachers" and "Defend rights"; and 4. "People should work for a living" and "Give to the needy.")

Form four groups. Give each group a numbered belief card. Read each of the following numbered situations to the group with corresponding numbers. For example, the group with belief card 1 would respond to situation 1. The situations are: 1. A friend wants you to help him cheat on a test; 2. Your parent asks you to lie; 3. A teacher unjustly accuses you of something you didn't do; and 4. A homeless person asks you for money.

Have each group read both sides of its belief card and decide how to respond to the situation. Then ask:

- **Was it difficult to decide what to do? Why or why not?**
- **What did you do when you were confused about which belief to act on?**

Say: **Sometimes our beliefs contradict each other. God's Word is our best source for figuring out how God wants us to live. It teaches us which belief is more important in confusing situations.**

The Bible Experience

Church of the Hypocrite?

(For this activity, you'll need Bibles, newsprint, tape, markers, slips of paper, and pencils.)

Say: **Hypocrisy—not living what you say you believe—isn't a new problem. In Revelation 2–3, Jesus confronts seven churches with their weaknesses and offers solutions.** Read aloud Revelation 2–3.

Form seven groups (one person may form a group.). Give each group a Bible, newsprint, and markers. Assign a different church from Revelation 2–3 to each group. Have groups each draw churches on their newsprint and write possible present-day actions of their assigned churches. For example, the church in Sardis might have some people who are lazy and sleep in all the time. Be available to help groups think of present-day applications.

When groups are finished, have them post their newsprint around the room. Then have kids walk around and look at all seven churches. Say: **God is displeased with hypocrisy. He wants us to have a pure faith—one where we live out what we believe. Let's take a look at excuses people use to not live out their beliefs. After I read an**

excuse, go stand by the church you think would've used that excuse.

Say: **The first excuse is: God won't mind if I do it just this once.** After kids have chosen churches, have them discuss these questions with the others who selected the same church. Ask:

● **Where or when are you tempted to use this type of excuse?**

● **What is wrong with this excuse? Explain.**

Have someone from each group briefly share the group's answers with the whole class. Then read the following excuses one at a time, repeating the question-and-answer segment each time.

● It's too hard to be a Christian.

● God's rules are old-fashioned.

● I want to do wrong more than I want to do right.

● God isn't interested in the details of my life.

● I don't want to lose my friends, so I'll do it.

● Everyone else is doing it.

After all the excuses have been read and discussed, distribute pencils and slips of paper. Have each person write on a slip of paper the excuse he or she is most tempted to use. Have kids keep their slips, and encourage them to refer to the slips when they're tempted to use excuses.

Reflection and Application

What I Believe

(For this activity, you'll need transparent tape, index cards of three different colors, a pencil, and a Bible for each person.)

Give each person three index cards of different colors, a pencil, and a Bible. Have kids write on each card one thing they believe about God and one way that belief has changed their life. For idea starters, have kids read Exodus 20; Deuteronomy 6; or John 1. Kids might write things such as "I believe God takes care of me, so I don't worry about things like money or food"; "I believe God wants me to do right, so I try to be honest"; or "I believe God loves all people, so I'm kind to people and I don't make fun of them."

Form groups of four, and have kids read their belief cards to each other. Then have groups each arrange their twelve belief cards in order of importance. After five minutes, have each group read aloud its top three cards. Then ask:

● **How difficult was it to rank your cards?**

● **How did you decide which beliefs were most important?**

● **Is it more important to just believe something or to use that belief in your actions?**

Ask group members to each tell which beliefs they'd be willing to die for. Then bring groups together. Have them tape their cards together to form a patchwork "quilt." Say: **Beliefs aren't a ranking system; they're more like an intersecting group of values that form a blanket of beliefs. We rest on and live by this blanket of beliefs.**

Choose Your Closing

❏ Option 1: Get in Touch With Reality

(For this activity, you'll need a blindfold and two small cups for each person. Fill half of the cups with room temperature cola and the other half with ice and cola.)

Blindfold kids, and have them each taste the cups of cola to decide which they prefer. Then ask:
● **Which cola did you like? Why?**
● **What is wrong with lukewarm cola?**
Have a volunteer read aloud Revelation 3:15-16. Ask:
● **Why does God prefer someone who is totally turned off to him to someone who is lukewarm to him?**
● **How would you describe a lukewarm Christian?**
● **What's wrong with a lukewarm Christian?**
● **Why would God want to spit the lukewarm Christian out instead of the cold one?**
Say: **Cold people understand that they're far from God, so they're more apt to come to God wholeheartedly. Lukewarm people think they're OK with God because they're doing some things right. Think about your own actions. Do they show that you're lukewarm, cold, or on fire for God?**
Close with prayer that kids will make the conscious decision to be on fire for God in their daily walks.

❏ Option 2: Authentic Label

Invite each person to take off an article of removable-in-front-of-a-group clothing. Have them read the clothing labels. Point out those that denote authenticity, such as "100% Cotton." Ask:
● **How would a label read for a Christian who lives his or her beliefs?**
Have kids who want to be 100 percent authentic in their Christian faith think of labels to describe the kind of Christians they want to be. For example, kids may say, "100 percent authentic Christian," "50 percent loving and 50 percent giving," or "50 percent strong and 50 percent striving—handle with care."
Have kids stand and tell what their labels are. Close in prayer, asking God to help kids live out their faith authentically.

Goal:
We are the church!

Scripture Verses:
Ephesians 4:3-16

The Ch_rch Needs U!

Our preteen kids aren't the "church of tomorrow." They're part of the church of today! It is today that they must learn their place in tomorrow's church—in attitude, in role, and in mission.

Use this lesson to help kids look at the characteristics they have in common with each other. Help them discover how they can use these qualities to serve in the church.

Choose Your Opening

❏ Option 1: Link Tag

(For this activity, you'll need a Bible.)

Select a person to be "It" for this game. This person will attempt to tag other participants. Once a participant is tagged, he or she will link elbows with It. The linked pair will then pursue other participants and repeat the process. The game is over when everyone is linked together.

Have a volunteer read aloud Ephesians 4:3-6 while the group is linked together. Then form groups of four or five, and have groups discuss the following questions:

● **How is this game like the church as it attempts to develop unity?**

● **At what point were the taggers weakest? strongest? Explain.**

● **How can our class be strong and unified?**

● **Why is it necessary for the church to be "one"?**

● **Is complete unity possible? Explain.**

Now play the game again. This time, have kids shout, "One Lord, one faith, one baptism" after they link elbows.

After everyone is linked, say: **During this lesson, we'll discover the importance of unity—and the strength of that unity—as a** church. You'll also learn that you have a valuable role in our church.

❏ Option 2: Team Up

(For this activity, you'll need a Bible.)

Have kids form teams by following your directions as you say the following statements:
- **Team up with others who have the same fingerprint as you!**
- **Team up with anyone who's related to you.**
- **Team up with those whose hair is a similar color to yours.**
- **Team up with anyone who shares a common interest or hobby with you.**
- **Team up with those who go to the same school as you.**
- **Team up with kids your own age.**
- **Team up with anyone wearing the same kind of shoes as you.**
- **Team up with anyone who's human!**

The final description should, obviously, create one large team. Read aloud Ephesians 4:3-6. Then form groups of four or five, and have groups discuss the following questions:
- **Which instructions made it difficult to form teams? Why?**
- **What made it so easy to form a team by following the last instruction?**
- **Is it possible for people to be different and yet maintain unity in the church? Explain.**
- **How did you feel when you successfully teamed up? When you didn't?**
- **Is the church ever like this? Why or why not?**

Say: **In this lesson we'll discover your role in our church—a church where you have both a place and a part.**

The Bible Experience

It's in the Cards

(For this activity, you'll need a deck of playing cards and a copy of the formula for every four or five people, a blindfold, and a Bible.)

Have kids form groups of four or five, and give each group a deck of playing cards and a copy of the following formula. Tell groups to shuffle the cards and deal the whole deck. Then have them determine individual roles for this game by using the formula.

Cards in Hand	Role	Action
The most Aces	You are the Mouth.	You are blindfolded. You can only repeat instructions supplied by the Eyes.
The most Kings	You are the Right Hand.	You must use your right hand alone. You can only listen to the Mouth's instructions. You may not speak.
The most Queens	You are the Left Hand.	You must use your left hand alone. You can only listen to the Mouth's instructions. You may not speak.
All others	You are the Eyes.	You can only inform the Mouth what to tell the Hands.

Once the roles are determined and understood, the Right Hand in each group will gather all the cards together. Read Ephesians 4:7-13 aloud, and say: **One of the roles of the church is to build up believers to maturity in Christ. It's time to "build up" your "body" and create a card house.**

Have groups attempt to build houses of cards using only the determined actions for their roles. After eight to ten minutes, have groups discuss the following questions:

● **Which role was most important to build the card house? Explain.**

● **Which role listed in Ephesians 4:11 (apostles, prophets, evangelists, pastors, or teachers) is most important? least important? Explain.**

● **How important is it that everyone is involved in a church?**

After several minutes of discussion, say: **Every Christian is called to serve the body of Christ in some way. Every part is valuable—from the eyes and ears to the tongue and feet. That's why *you* are so important.**

Common Mission, Uncommon Ministry

(For this activity, you'll need paper, pencils, and a Bible.)

Remain in the groups from the "It's in the Cards" activity, or form new groups of four or five. Give each group paper and pencils. Have one group member draw four columns on the paper and write each of the following category titles at the top of each column: Interests or Hobbies, Backgrounds or History, Abilities or Skills, and Miscellaneous.

Tell groups they'll have four minutes to brainstorm common bonds that they share with fellow group members, one minute for each of the areas listed. Nothing is too outlandish. Groups should especially identify items that all group members hold in common.

After four minutes, have groups each review their lists and answer the following question:

● **How can we, as a class, use these common bonds for ministry within our church?**

Encourage groups to be as creative (yet realistic) as possible. Then vote as a large group on which missions you'll complete in the following year. Read Ephesians 4:14-16, and say: **A united church is a powerful church: powerful in vision, powerful in ministry, and powerful in effectiveness. When we are divided, we are weak. When we are united with God and each other, we are strong.**

Choose Your Closing

❏ Option 1: Bricks

(For this activity, you'll need a brick and a permanent marker for each person.)

Form pairs, and give each person a brick and a permanent marker. Each person will write on his or her brick one way he or she will become involved in the local church (this could be a service opportunity, a part of the church ministry, or the gift of an individual skill or ability). Partners should share with each other any potential obstacles to getting involved and then pray for one another.

After several minutes, invite the kids to openly share their desired avenues of service and place their bricks in a group wall. Close in prayer, asking God for wisdom and strength to accomplish these mighty acts of service.

❏ Option 2: Church Walk

Take everyone on a tour of your church. In various rooms and areas, stop and point out opportunities in which kids might become involved. Possible areas include: the altar, the worship center, the choir loft, the janitor's closet, the kitchen, the sound booth, the nursery, and the church library.

Move quickly, and encourage kids to share their thoughts about service opportunities. When you're finished with the tour, form pairs, and invite each person to commit to one specific church ministry or opportunity he or she will become involved in. Then close in prayer.

Your Serve!

Preteen kids are about to leave a stage of life where just about everything is done for them. They're starting to understand that the Christian life means servanthood—being more concerned about what we do for others than what we do for ourselves. This lesson will help kids see that Jesus gave us the ultimate example of servanthood.

Choose Your Opening

❏ Option 1: Waiter!

(For this activity, you'll need a pad of paper and a pencil as a prize.)

Have kids sit in a circle. Say: **You're all waiters at Churchy's Restaurant. One at a time, I'd like you to say your name and one food item you want. Next, each of you will try to repeat, in order, everyone's names and food orders. For each name and food order you get right, you'll receive a point, or a "tip."**

Play the game. Have kids count the names and food items they remembered. Award a pad of paper and a pencil to the waiter who remembered the most. Then ask:

● **Was it easy or difficult to remember the names and food orders? Explain.**

● **How was this game like or unlike serving others? Explain.**

Say: **Good servants remember the needs of those they serve. We'll learn more about servanthood in today's lesson.**

❏ Option 2: The Right Order

(For this activity, prepare eleven sheets of paper with each letter of the word "servanthood" written on a separate sheet. Using the sheets in the same order, write with a different-colored marker the letters in the words "last is first" on the back sides of the sheets. You'll also need tape.)

Line up the kids, and randomly tape a sheet of paper to each of their

► Extra! Extra!
If you have a small group, make the game more challenging by having kids say their names and two or three food items.

backs so that one of the letters in the word "servanthood" is showing. Say: **Arrange yourselves so the letters on your backs spell one word. No talking, please.**

When kids have come up with the word, ask:

● **How did it feel to help one another line up in the right order?**

● **How was this game like servanthood?**

Then say: **Stay in your line, and help the person beside you by taking the letter off his or her back and turning it over. Tape it back on with the new letter showing. Provide more tape if kids need it.** Now ask:

● **What words are spelled now?**

● **What do these words have to do with servanthood?**

Say: **During this meeting, we'll learn that Jesus showed us how to be servants and he wants us to help others be "first."**

The Bible Experience

Up and Running

(For this activity, prepare a large piece of newsprint by writing on it the words "Anything you did for even the least of my people here, you also did for me," from Matthew 25:40b. Have a Bible available.)

Have a volunteer read Matthew 25:31-40. Ask:

● **What does this passage say about servanthood?**

Say: **Serving God is more than giving money to church or participating in service projects. As Jesus said, "Anything you did for even the least of my people here, you also did for me."**

Show kids the newsprint with the words from Matthew 25:40b. Tell kids they're going to build a "machine." Ask one person to say the first word of the verse, "Anything," over and over while making a motion, such as nodding his or her head. Then ask another person to somehow link up to the first person, say the second word of the verse, "you," right after the first person says "anything," and create a different motion to repeat over and over. Continue to build the machine with kids adding actions and words. If you have less than sixteen kids, have some kids say more than one word. If you have more than sixteen kids, have some kids double up on words.

Let the completed machine run for thirty seconds. Then have the kids try fast motion. Finally, have the machine slow down and come to a complete stop. Then ask:

● **How did you feel as you added your part of the machine?**

● **How did you feel when the machine was finally complete?**

● **How is this like the way we serve each other?**

Just Do It!

(For this activity, you'll need a sheet of paper, a pencil, and an envelope for each person.)

Give each person a sheet of paper, a pencil, and an envelope. Say: **Some of you may have heard of New Year's resolutions. You may even have made one or two. Today we're going to get a fresh start on our attitudes toward serving others by writing "serve-solutions."**

Have kids write three serve-solutions they'll complete within the next month—one that's fun ("I'll see a movie with my four-year-old brother"); one that's a little bit of work ("I'll help Mr. Smith shovel his sidewalk for free"); and one that's a bit tougher ("I'll volunteer one night a week at the nursing home").

Have kids write their names on the outsides of their envelopes, insert their serve-solutions in the envelopes, and seal them. Collect the envelopes, and tell kids you'll hand them out again in a month so kids can check on how they're doing. Then ask:

● **Was it easy or difficult to think of ways to serve? Explain.**

● **Do the things you already do to serve others fall into the "fun" category, the "bit of work" category, or the "tough" category? Explain.**

● **Keeping in mind the Bible verse you studied earlier** (Matthew 25:40b), **how seriously will you try to accomplish your serve-solutions?**

Choose Your Closing

❏ Option 1: Your Serve!

(For this activity, you'll need a Bible, a badminton racket and shuttle-cock, a trash can, and a sign that reads "Great Serve!" Tape the sign to the trash can.)

Have someone read Matthew 20:25-28. Then ask:

● **What does Jesus tell us about servanthood?**

Say: **Jesus commissions us to serve others, and he practices what he preaches. Think of some ways we can practice what Jesus preaches.**

Have kids each tell one of their serve-solutions and then try to "serve" the badminton shuttlecock into the trash can. Each time a person makes a goal, have everyone yell, "Great serve!" Make it easier by having

everyone stand around the trash can and help the shuttlecock into the trash can.

Ask kids to form a circle around the trash can. Close with a prayer, asking for God's help to serve others.

❏ Option 2: Forever and Ever, Amen!

(For this activity, you'll need a Bible.)

Ask kids what "infinity" means. Show them that the sign for infinity is like the figure 8. Have kids stand in a figure 8 and join hands. Then say: **Jesus' love is endless. He is ready to serve us, providing never-ending encouragement and strength as we serve others.**

Go around the figure 8, and let each person share a serve-solution. Close in prayer, asking for God's help to serve others and thanking God for his everlasting encouragement and love. Read Matthew 28:20 as an amen.

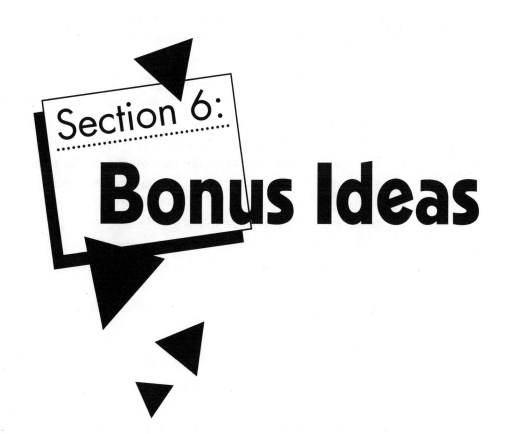

Section 6:
Bonus Ideas

Kids are bombarded with "if it feels good, do it" thinking. They need to know that they can make a difference in the world around them—both now and in the future. They need to understand that they can use their time, talents, and abilities to serve God and others.

Preteen kids like to serve others and to feel useful. Service projects have immediate and future benefits for the kids, their leaders and parents, and the people or organizations they help.

With proper preparation on the part of leaders, kids will

● become more aware of people, places, and problems at home and in the community;

● work together to accomplish a task;

● meet needs not seen in their "me-centered" world;

● become more aware of others, including the elderly, the ill, the homeless, or the poor; and

● practice the art of service in the name of Christ.

Plan It Right

Do your research. Check out needs in your own church, in the neighborhood surrounding your church, at service organizations in your community, and in business areas that kids frequent. Network with other leaders, youth directors, and affiliated agencies that work to meet needs in your area.

Dig a little deeper. After identifying areas your kids can work in, find out exactly what the needs are. Visit the neighborhoods, malls, agency facilities, or ministries within your church.

Schedule kids' service. Set firm dates and times to serve, and arrange for adult supervision and assistance in advance. Prepare kids by discussing the types of service they will be doing and sharing a devotional to direct their thoughts about why we serve.

Stay involved. When kids minister on a regular basis—with consistency—they'll see the continuing benefits of their ministry. Don't be surprised if you and your kids begin to view the world in a whole new way. Coming face to face with human need and doing something about it can be a truly transformational experience!

25 Kid-Friendly Service Projects

In Your Church

Sign Designers

Have kids cheer up the church custodian, encourage the choir members, or delight an elderly church member at a nursing home by making signs or banners to share their appreciation and the love of Jesus.

Galley Crew

Have kids reach out to needy and ill people in the congregation with a home-cooked meal. Form groups of kids to prepare the main course, side dishes, delicious desserts, and a creative presentation for this special meal. Set up delivery times, and have kids sing songs of praise as they make someone's day a special event.

I'm Praying for You

Have kids surprise someone in your church with an anonymous note saying: "I'm your prayer person for this month. God bless you!" Let each person choose one congregation member and commit to praying daily for him or her for the next month.

Yard-Care Crews

Form teams of kids to pull weeds, plant flowers, rake leaves, mow lawns, and sweep the grounds of your church or the headquarters of a local service agency. Provide the equipment, and then surprise the workers with pizza or ice cream after a hard day of work.

In Your Neighborhood

Doorbell Ditch

Have kids think of gifts that people in their neighborhood would enjoy receiving, such as flowers, small meals, candy, or cookies. Send kids out with these gifts, and tell them to leave the gifts on the doorsteps, ring the doorbells, and run! Attach brief notes that say "God loves you, and so do we!" Include the name of your church or preteen group on the notes.

Kids' Blockbuster Block Party

Have preteen kids organize, advertise, and host a party for younger neighborhood kids. Decorate a room at church or the garage of one of your kids' homes. Play games, sing songs, and eat! Here is a time for neighbors to enjoy a "time off." If children bring donations, give the money to a children's home or adoption agency.

Follow That Truck

Take kids out early to scour the neighborhood after the garbage trucks have "done their thing." Pick up missed trash, and carefully stand the trash cans by the side of the road. Don't forget the lids!

Breakfast Shop

Have kids surprise the neighborhood trash collectors by meeting them with a hot curb-side breakfast or cookies and coffee if it's later in the day. Be sure to have food in "to go" containers in case workers can't stay to finish the meal. This would also work with other city workers—mail carriers, public utility workers, or crossing guards at elementary schools.

At Home

Brother's or Sister's Chores

Kids can complete an act of kindness at home by doing chores for their siblings without saying a word. An only child can do chores for his or her parents. When asked, "What's going on?" kids can simply respond, "I love you, and so does Jesus!"

Cookie Giveaway

Plan a party for your preteen kids to make cookies and then give them away! A plateful of cookies for the family is a real treat. Or surprise the pastor, neighbors, teachers, or low-income families who live near your church.

Season Servants

Adapt this to fit your climate and the time of year. Have kids reach out—to their families, to their neighbors, to the elderly, or to the community—by caring for people's yards. In the fall, bring rakes and leaf blowers to tidy yards and brooms to sweep out the gutters. In the winter, bring shovels to clear off snowy sidewalks and rock salt to spread on icy steps. In the spring, do some weeding and plant flowers. In the summer, mow and water lawns.

Good Morning, Folks

Have kids make cassette-tape greetings to brighten someone's day. Have kids place the cassette by the recipient's car keys and leave a note saying, "Play this tape to start your day right!"

Play this to start your day!

In the Community

Runners' Relief

Station kids along the local park's running trail offering free drinks of Gatorade or lemonade to anyone who is thirsty. Or set up a stand to offer free drinks to busy shoppers downtown or at the mall. Tape a poster to the stand that includes your church's name and address.

Drop-in Visits

Encourage kids to drop by the local nursing home and inquire at the receptionist's desk if anyone might enjoy having a visitor. Also have kids ask what they might bring to share with the residents. Remind kids to be polite as they tell about themselves and ask about the residents' families.

Bag Man

Take kids to a busy shopping center. They can help carry packages to cars, get "rent a strollers" ready for kids, and help with directions to stores, restaurants, and restrooms.

Kid Care

Have kids provide a baby-sitting service for frazzled shoppers, free of charge. Go to the mall or a downtown shopping area and take coloring books, crayons, games, clay, and toys. Provide "Shopper Shows" for kids (and tired adults) with prepared skits and puppet shows. Be sure to get proper authorization from mall or city authorities.

For Those in Need

Get It Together

Have kids organize donations given to agencies by cleaning and sorting giveaway clothing or arranging the canned and boxed goods in a food pantry.

On Stage

Have kids perform puppet shows, musicals, concerts, or choir performances at shelters, soup kitchens, or hospices. Let the kids organize and produce the show. Add some fun by bringing along lots of popcorn and passing it out in lunch bags during the show.

Oh, Waiter!

Have kids help prepare and serve the food at a soup kitchen or hospice. There's work for everyone, including setup, tear down, and the dreaded cleanup!

Helping Hands

The kids can get "down and dirty" cleaning up the yard of a local shelter to spruce the place up. Have kids paint furniture, walls, or items that don't need to be "perfect."

Mail Call

Have the kids help prepare a bulk mailing or promote a fund-raiser to benefit a service agency. Kids could help with similar tasks at your own church, too.

Breakfast of Champions

Ask kids to donate a few dollars to buy fast-food breakfasts to give away. Locate an area in your city where the homeless often sleep. Go there early in the morning to deliver breakfast to the homeless.

Tree Trimmers

With a bit of legwork, your group can reach a needy family at holiday time. Through a local service agency, obtain the names, needs, and clothing sizes of a family who may not be able to afford clothing or gifts for their young children at Christmas.

Have the kids use red or green markers to write each needed item on an index card. Punch a hole in each card and thread it with a ribbon. Hang cards on a Christmas tree located where your congregation can easily access it. Encourage each member of the congregation to select and take one card, purchase and wrap the item listed, and place the gift under the Christmas tree. When the items have been collected, kids can work with the agency to deliver the gifts.

Terrific Tagging

Your kids can work with the local authorities to wipe out graffiti messes. Have a team of kids willing to go out when needed to paint over the messes that "taggers" leave on fences, walls, and buildings.

Special Friends

Your group can have lots of fun, learn a bunch, and help people of all ages by volunteering to help at the nearest Special Olympics. The excitement and joy of participants and spectators is sure to rub off on your willing workers.

Evaluation of *NO-MISS LESSONS FOR PRETEEN KIDS*

Please help Group Publishing, Inc., continue to provide innovative and usable resources for ministry by taking a moment to fill out and send us this evaluation. Thanks!

● ● ●

1. As a whole, this book has been (circle one):

Not much help   Very helpful

1   2   3   4   5   6   7   8   9   10

2. The things I liked best about this book were:

3. This book could be improved by:

4. One thing I'll do differently because of this book is:

5. Optional Information:

Name_____

Street Address _____

City_____ State _____Zip _____

Phone Number _____Date_____